Acknowledgements

Because of the tremendous impact the great "I AM" has had on my life, I just cannot say thanks to anyone before Him.

To my totally committed, fantastic, supportive, and beautiful wife I say a very, very special thank you.

To my children who challenge me continually and draw the best from me, I say thanks for your love and support.

To The Nova Group community of people who encouraged me and helped me with ideas and suggestions, I say many thanks.

To all the scholars, writers, motivational speakers, and ministers that contributed by teaching me something, I must say thanks.

Caleb/Ches,

I love you with more than a natural father's love, you have great potential for the Kingdom of God & I look forward to seeing you fulfill it.

lots DAD
xoxo

Contents

Foreword i

Introduction iii

1. Understanding "I AMness" 1

2. The Objectives of "I AM" 11

3. The "I AM" That Is God 19

4. Sonship and "I AM" 29

5. Jesus, The "I AM" 39

6. The "I AM" That Are Sons 49

7. The Thoughts of "I AM" 59

8. The Words of "I AM" 67

9. The Attitude of "I AM" 77

10. I AM The Finished Product 85

Foreword

I am so proud of my husband living out one of his dreams by writing and publishing this book. He has written from his heart with the enthusiasm and hope that each one who reads it will be impacted by the very depths and heights of the revelation of I AMness.

In understanding and living out the principle of I AM, barriers and hindrances to growth in our lives are removed. There are no limits to the opportunities that we are presented with to live a fruitful and overcoming life. Making the Right Choices, assured that we can, guarantees that we shall accomplish all that God has purposed for us, thereby fulfilling our Destiny.

Accepting our I AMness delivers us from the bondages of fear-of-the-unknown and liberates us to be in a constant, moment-by-moment state of BEing whereby we open ourselves continually to change and learning new things, thereby releasing the Power of God (The Great I AM) through and from our lives into others, our surroundings, and our circumstances.

I trust that you, the reader, will open up your mind and heart to the imminent expansion in your life as you read, meditate on, and allow what Brent has written to start you, or continue you, or bring you into the culmination of a search for Perfection, the Perfection in human form that propels you into knowing and living: "I AM, therefore I CAN!"

Christine Jackson-Hart

Introduction

As you approach this book, *I AM, Therefore I CAN*, and this topic, please keep an open mind. The principle and power of I AM is meant to motivate you and make you better and take you higher. Life comes in "cans" and I AM can turn your "I cannot" into "I can." If you are satisfied with who and what you are, and your accomplishments and your contributions to life absolutely fulfill you, then you might not need this book. If the opposite is true, then read on and be objective: the potential to be a better you is right before you. I AM certain of this: you can.

Understanding is absolutely important to the development of life; however, we can have our own understanding of things and they can be totally erroneous. We can believe a lot of things in life, and we do, but believing something does not make it right. There are many who hold to the belief that what they believe is the right thing, and most times their belief is not founded on any substantial investigation or evidence. You can be sincere while being sincerely wrong. It is my prayer and hope that something in this book, however small, might impact you and challenge you to embrace, implement, and release your I AM, all that you can do, and consequently your God-given destiny.

I know once we see the word "God" we think religion. "God" is not about religion but about life, so please when you approach this book, dismiss religion entirely and give the ideas and principles here a chance to improve your life. Yes they can.

Many times I challenge people as to what they believe, its foundation, its ability to produce, and the evidence of their belief system being something worth more than a religious belief, theory, or traditional rhetoric. There are always three sides to a story; there is yours, there is mine, and then there is the truth. My objective here is not to be right about everything, but to challenge for change to the things that I have seen practiced without effective results. Things can change.

We live in a world and an era, age, and season that presents us with many options for improvement. While I see much advance in technology and many other areas of life, it seems to me that man as a being in general is not particularly showing much improvement in his behavioral patterns. The barbaric nature that man seems to be manifesting throughout his history continues (it might even be getting worse), only disguised in a more modern form, with more sophisticated weapons. We can change that.

The I AM principle is not a religious law, but it is a spiritual principle that can transform a life and consequently other lives, families, communities, and nations. It all starts with you. You can continue your present I AM's and continue to reap the same old same old, or you can change your I AM's and totally transform your life and your world. You can change.

Connecting with the great I AM was a memorable day in my life and one I will never forget or stop giving testimony of. After that, I spent many years in what I referred to as a personal relationship with I AM, but nothing compares to the dimension of fellowship that I now experience. Understanding, embracing, and implementing I AM will catapult you from where you presently are to where you are meant to be. I AM is the missing ingredient you have longed for but has long eluded you. Your "I can" is directly linked to your I AM.

The essence of this book is to release the power of the connectivity that is between God and man. Religion gives you programs and methods to appease God; I AM gives you principles for connecting and manifesting God. The I AM principle is the releasing of the God that is IN you and the God that you are INto.

I AM has the potential to radically change your life forever.

I AM totally convinced, I AM certain, I AM sure, I AM expecting it from you.

Yes you can, yes we can.

Chapter One
Understanding "I AMness"

THE ULTIMATE KEY TO YOUR SUCCESS

*"Trust in the Lord with all your heart
and lean not on your own understanding."*

<u>INDIVIDUALITY and "I AM"</u>

While "understanding" is absolutely important in every area of life, it is imperative to note that our "own understanding" can be inaccurate and/or erroneous and therefore not beneficial to our development and/or progress.

Many of us are way more comfortable being a "we" rather than an "I." We look to others to make us complete; consequently, we are less of the "I" that we are meant to be. Maybe the responsibility of being an "I" is just too much, so we would rather be a "we" and have another to share the blame/responsibility if or when we "mess up."

Take, for example, in marriage, where traditionally a spouse is referred to as the "other (or better) half" rather than understanding that marriage is the union of two whole, singular individuals and not

~ I AM therefore I CAN ~

two halves. Instead of thinking of marriage in the context of "addition" (as one PLUS one equals two), we must see it as multiplication: one MULTIPLIED by one equaling One (couple) and becoming One (in vision and purpose), yet each maintaining his/her uniqueness.

While it is a fact that we all need others to contribute to and even enhance our development (and certainly for many other reasons), I, as a singular individual, AM endowed with all that I need in order to function effectively! This fact is the essence of understanding I AM and the existence of one single, individual, complete person, even when joined to another in marriage. We must maintain our individuality at all times.

I is first person singular, *ego* is the Greek word for "I," I is first person, I is singular; too much "I," or "singular-ness," and one can be considered egotistical, or be called an "I" specialist. "I" must be kept in the right context and perspective. I AM is the first person singular, present tense form of the main verb, in English, "to be." AM is the first person singular, present tense of BE. I AM can very well be translated "I BE." AM/BE can also mean "to exist." *Exist* is a derivative of the word "existence," which is the state of living.

In the most straightforward definition then, the simple English word AM means what one individual, singular person BE, is presently being, or lives BEing.

What I AM, I BE.

I AM is the very essence of God, "I" being personal and singular, and "AM" being present.

God stands alone, as supreme, or else God would be equal to or subject to others. God therefore being in lone supremacy cannot be subject to place or time; He is past, present, and future and everywhere, all at the same time. He is the most powerful single individual in time and space, not needing any other in order to become whole or complete, nor relying on another to be fulfilled or become a "we," most assuredly The Great I AM.

~ Understanding "I AMness" ~

I AM CONNECTIVITY

I AM can only be fully realized when one is connected or linked to the great I AM. I AM must have its roots in an I AM that is greater than ourselves (God), and one capable of providing the results expected from the implementation of I AMness. This is not religion or religious belief; this is in fact the relationship from which all other relationships are patterned. The biblical personalities John the Baptist and Jesus Christ understood this principle, and hence they were linked to the great I AM and as a result fulfilled their own I AMness.

Any successful I AMness must flow from the understanding of the I AM relationship, as Jesus said in John 17:21; "that they all be one as You Father are in Me and I in You, that they also be one in Us that the world will believe that you sent Me." In verse 23 He says, "I in them and You in Me, that they be made perfect in one…" This is completed unity, this is true oneness, this is I AM connectivity. It is this unity that creates and sustains I AMness and shows the world who Jesus Christ is, the manifesting of Christ through mankind here on earth. Actually, the true spiritual depth of this is recorded in Galatians 2:20: "I have been crucified with Christ, it is no longer I who lives but Christ who lives IN me; and the life I now live in the flesh I live by faith in the Son of God, who loved me and gave Himself for me." The truth is that your I AM is really totally connected to the I AM that is Jesus Christ, being lived out through you and me. In 2 Corinthians 13:5 it says, "Examine yourselves as to whether you are in the faith. Test yourselves. Do you not know yourselves, that Jesus Christ is IN you? Unless you fail the test and are disqualified." I AMness has its roots, its substance, its life, and consequently its fulfillment in being united with the great I AM. All other things are empty, superficial, temporary forms of I AMness.

Numerous times in scripture we are told that our bodies are the temple of God. In Acts 7:48 Stephen says, "The Most High does not dwell in temples made with hands." Paul reiterates that fact to some Greek philosophers in Acts 17:24. Then there is this; "Do you not know that you are the temple of God and that the Spirit of God dwells IN you? If anyone defiles the temple of God, God will destroy him for the temple of God is holy and you are that temple" (1 Corinthians 3:16-17). And again further on in 6:19, "Do you not know that your body is the temple of the Holy Spirit who is IN you, whom you have from God…" The only place God lives on this earth is IN those who are connected to Him. Your I AM, and consequently your "I can," is only possible through connectivity with the great I AM.

"I AM" IDENTITY

When someone approaches me and asks, "Are you Brent Hart?" I can simply answer, "I AM" or "I AM not." I cannot answer "I AM" if they refer to me by another name. It must be the name by which I AM called and known, the name with which I AM identified. "I AM" must be in response to the BEing that I AM, the individual that I AM, the singular person that I AM. The truth, though, is that answering "I AM" to my name is way short of the real I AM that I AM. Names are very powerful in individual empowerment, in association, and for calling forth one's particular destiny; however, a name is just a name if not linked to the I AM that goes way deeper than a name.

In Hebrew thinking, a name must give a person purpose and function. Solomon means peace and his reign as king over Israel was a peaceful period. Joseph named his first son Manasseh, which means forgiveness and represents his forgiveness of his brothers for selling him into slavery.

Take the name Jesus, which means "God is Salvation," then link it to Christ which means "The Anointed One." It is a powerful name to be: God is Salvation, The Anointed One, but only when character is linked to a name can we achieve success. A name is only a name unless it is given the dynamics necessary to fulfill the power of the name; the power of a name is fulfilled through character. These are the deeper attributes and characteristics of which Jesus the Christ spoke and lived to fulfill His I AMness.

~ Understanding "I AMness" ~

He, Jesus Christ, the individual with this powerful name, was tempted in every way as all men are, yet He did not sin (Hebrews 4:15). There was ample opportunity for Him to live up to the name or fail to live up to it. He constantly made the right choices, thereby succeeding at accomplishing His I AMness to perfection. In other words, you can have a powerful name and miss the boat by not applying the added ingredients necessary to fulfill your name and achieve your personal I AMness.

RELEASING "I AM"

The BEing that I AM goes way beyond what one sees or hears, though, of course, what one sees and hears from me will represent the person that I "Be" but not always necessarily the person that I AM. The person that I AM being at any given time could very well be due to erroneous training and may fall way short of the person that I AM destined to be. While "I AM" and "I BE" are the same and interchangeable, "I BE" is predominantly present while "I AM" is present and future. My point is that the person that I AM is usually quite buried beneath the person that I have been socialized, cultured, formed, and shaped to be and AM consequently presently being.

For most of us, our true I AM is latent and waiting for the release of the realization that all that I can and will be is presently with me as I AM.

All that I AM meant to be, all that I AM to become, all that I AM to fulfill, all that I AM designed and destined for, is all presently with me and truly who I AM. However, understanding this and releasing this now is the key to its fulfillment.

TRUE "I AM"

In understanding "I Amness," please let us be sure we are not talking about the ego, arrogance, and insecurity of many individuals. There are many who when given a little position in life are quick to run around spouting off, "Do you know who I AM?" No, we are talking about a serious, secure response to the power and effectiveness of the use of I AMness to accomplish successfully in life.

When I talk of "I AMness," I fully understand also that there are many explanations out there that will be contrary to my definition or to how I interpret or explain this word or phrase. Nevertheless, for the sake of understanding the bigger picture of which I have only just begun to paint, please allow my personal definition and explanation to suffice for the present.

While we focus on and grasp an understanding of "I AMness," let us all be sure we also understand the power of "I AM NOTness." While one must be confident and sure about who they are and what their purpose and destiny is, they should equally be sure of that which it is not. John the Baptist was just such a person. When asked who he was, "Are you the Christ, Elijah, etc.?" John was adamant to respond, "I AM not." He concluded, however, with saying who he was in John 1:23: "I AM 'the voice of one crying in the wilderness: Make straight the way of the Lord,' as the prophet Isaiah said." John is a person who knew who he was and who he was not, and, I might add, quite secure in both. This is very important because this will directly determine what you can do and what you cannot do.

John went on to say further on in John 3:27, "A man can receive nothing unless it has been given to him from heaven." He understood I AMness while also understanding I AM NOTness.

> "I AM, WHEN FULFILLED, IS SONSHIP
> REALIZED AND DESTINY ACHIEVED."

I AMness is really about oneness with the great I AM. Let us look at the words of prayer Jesus spoke in John 17:20-23: "I do not pray for these alone but also for those who would believe in Me through their word. That they all may be one as You Father are IN Me and I IN You, that they also may be one IN Us, that the world may believe that You sent Me; and the glory which You gave Me I have given them, that they may be one just as We are one. I IN them and You IN

Me that they may be made perfect IN one and that the world may know that You have sent Me and have loved them as you have loved Me."

"I AM" FAITH

Given the present tense of the word AM, it speaks of the now, not what was before or what will be after, but the now. I AM speaks to the very present now, that which is before you now; it must be a very present existing situation that you will rightly respond "I AM" to. However, that which is the future can warrant an "I AM" response when one understands the dynamics of faith. This is not faith as connected to any religious practice, not faith as linked to a "faith based organization" (a new buzz term), not faith used generally as a cliché. Here I am speaking of the dynamics of faith, true faith, faith that produces, faith that delivers.

It is in this context that we can understand why Jesus Christ is referred to as the author/chief leader and perfecter/finisher of faith in Hebrews 12:2. He was the perfect example of one living out their I AMness in the now, by faith. Jesus lived out His I AM through who He was being at every moment. His declarations and proclamations concerning Himself were all words mixed with the character of His future I AMness that was being drawn into the present. I AMness in its truest form is the release and manifestation of Sonship.

Understanding the power of what we say, the power of our speech, or the power of our tongue is vital for faith to deliver our "I AMness." For example, "The power of life and death is in the tongue and they that love it would eat the fruit of it" (Proverbs 18:21). Many will quote this proverb but fail to understand the real power of the spoken word and consequently the fruit of it. There is most definitely death or life in everything the tongue says.

Do we really understand that God, the great I AM, spoke this entire universe into being? All that we now see, all that is part of this material tangible world, earth, and universe is the result of some words. Then there is The Word in the beginning with God and The Word being God Himself, then The Word becoming flesh and making His dwelling among mankind. Understanding I AMness is fundamental to understanding the power of what we say and the fact that all of creation has ears. Yes, I said ears not exactly ears like we have sticking out of our heads, but everything in creation can hear and therefore respond to the resonance of our words.

> "I AM, WHEN SPOKEN AND LIVED,
> HAS THE POTENTIAL TO CREATE."

God spoke to mountains, rivers, seas, and ravines. Jesus spoke to a fig tree and everything that was opposed to His destiny. We are told if we say to a mountain or a tree to move to another location, it can obey us (see Matthew 17:20). One would conclude that it is obvious they can all hear. A centurion once said to Jesus, "you don't need to change your location, just speak the word and my servant will be healed" (Matthew 8:8). Even far off from where the word was being spoken, the illness had the ability to hear. So too our future, which might be far off but can hear the word of I AM spoken in the present.

Remember I said that true faith is faith that produces, faith that delivers. Faith is being absolutely sure, confident, and of the persuasion that what is not now will be, and what is not now seen will be seen with the application of faith (Hebrews 11:1). Faith is being persuaded and confident that you can. Faith is applied through speech and action. We get into a car, a plane, or any vehicle for that matter, and we announce that we are going to a particular destination. How many of us realize the faith we put in an aircraft and its crew to take us where we are not able to carry ourselves ? We live lives of faith constantly; every chair we sit in, without inspecting it, we put confidence and trust in that it can accommodate us.

From that perspective of faith, one can respond with "I AM" to a future situation. What is not now being seen or accomplished but is absolutely sure to be seen and accomplished is the dynamic of faith that allows you to speak "I AM" in a now present situation. What you speak you will see come to pass, I am sure of it; look out for it

~ Understanding "I AMness" ~

that's the dynamic of faith of which I speak.

No wonder scripture tells us that without faith it is impossible to please God (Hebrews 11:6).

<u>Speaking "I AM" to a future situation has the power to bring into the present that situation as you see it to be, expect it to be, and work it to be. I AMness has the capacity to pull your future into the present and put life and existence to what is not now present.</u>

"I AM" TIMING

Kenny Rogers sang a song called "I AM the Greatest" about a little boy playing baseball, and while he is learning the game he says, "I AM the greatest there has ever been." The last two verses say, "I AM the greatest that's a fact, but even I didn't know I could pitch like that, I AM the greatest that is understood but even I didn't know I could pitch that good." That's a cool example of understanding I AMness and timing. We will see it when we declare it.

There is also a well-known boxer formally called Cassius Clay who utilized his I AM to enhance his boxing career: "I AM the greatest, I said that even before I knew I was" (Muhammad Ali).

I AMness, while more central to the present and the future, in its very essence also includes the past. I AMness really has no time frame, no date and hour and minutes; I AMness goes beyond the boundaries and limits of time as we know it. We can do nothing about the past except learn from it, we cannot undo it, we cannot change it, it has already happened and the consequences are already in play. What we can do is cut from the past and not allow the past to set up our present and in turn influence our future. There are many things we can learn from past experiences, circumstances, events, and situations that can enhance our present, and we should therefore do exactly that. However, the things that were wrong, the files that were corrupted, the viruses that caused us destruction and harm, they can be pulled up and deleted. Of course there must be a replacement of the old with that which is right.

The present, however, is quite different because the present is the future of the past. In the grand scheme of things, all things are future because as we speak, the present is delivering us to and connecting us to the future. Yet, the future is subject to the present because the one leads to the other and is therefore dependent on what is now to create what will be. In a real sense, the essence of all that we are is omnipresent. It is the "I AM that I AM."

I do not know if Kenny Rogers, the boy in his song, or Muhammad Ali know who I AM is, as Almighty God, or if they understand the principle of connectivity. Life is larger and lasts a lot longer than songs and sports. What I do know is, to BE what you want to BE is dependent on you thinking, speaking, and applying the I AMness principle through connectivity with the great I AM. Understand it, embrace it, and implement it; your life will never be the same. You can do it.

One writer summarizes it this way: "We need to understand that when we received salvation and were born again, we did not join a social club or a world religion called Christianity. We were regenerated and inhabited by a supernatural God who came to mingle with our spirit and transform us into a new creature with a heavenly nature, the very DNA of God now residing in us!"

My summary is taken from 1 John 5:20: *"We know also that the Son of God has come and has given us understanding, so that we may know Him who is true. And we are IN Him who is true—even IN His Son Jesus Christ. He is the true God and eternal life."*

I AMness is an "In" thing and leads us to an "I can" place.

Chapter Two
The Objectives of "I AM"

<u>"I AM" HAS THE POTENTIAL
TO TAKE YOU TO YOUR DESTINY.</u>

"To everything there is a season,
a time for every purpose under heaven."

PERSONAL FULFILLMENT

Like anything else in life, there must be an objective to achieve, a goal to work towards; it is the only way we will be motivated to overcome the obstacles and challenges we face in life. I AM has its own personal objectives with regard to the person applying the principle. The objectives of I AM will differ from person to person, we do not all have the same needs; therefore, we will not all have the same objectives. We all have some dream, some goal we are longing for, something we need desperately to fulfill, which you can with I AM.

If the question was asked, "Are you totally happy with where you are right now in life?" Most if not all will answer, if they are honest, a resounding "NO." We all fall short of all that we can be, hope to be, and want to be, but we can change that and improve. We can all move ourselves up from our present position. I AM totally convinced that the I AM principle, when truly understood, with the objectives of I AM implemented and of course continued, will put your destiny on its way to fulfillment.

The objectives of I AM are actually quite simple. I AM has as its goal delivering you to where you are meant to be, taking you to being the person you are destined to be. The objectives of I AM are to bring you to a place of fulfillment, completion, and perfection, to a place of being the finished product you are destined to be. I AM is the vehicle to your realizing your personal blueprint. I AM is just prior to your "I can."

DESTINY

As is in all of life, the negative of this principle is of course also true and unfortunately ignorantly applied by many unknowingly.

There are many parents who insist and persist in making negative declarations over their children. They refer to their children as being stupid, foolish, dumb, etc. If throughout my life all I hear is "I AM stupid," "I AM a fool," and "I AM dumb," give me a few years of that and I will speak and behave as though I AM stupid, I AM foolish, and I AM dumb. Destiny is wrapped up in I AM; it is our choice to be sure our destiny is a positive one.

To get to any destination or arrive at an objective in life, one must first know where one's destination is, or what one's objective is. There are a surprising amount of people on this planet that are without destination or objective, and yet they are trucking along as if they do know where or what their goal is. While there are many objectives that can be achieved in life, the objective of I AM surpasses them all. Because your "I can" follows your "I AM," then I AM is the ultimate objective.

I think of the apostle Paul speaking in Acts to the intellectual Greek philosophers and saying to them about God, "In Him we Live and

~ The Objectives of "I AM" ~

Move and have our being" (Acts 17:28). Wow, in God we have *Zoe*, which is "life and breath," in God we *Kineo*, which is "we move, we go, we are in motion," in God we have our *Esmen*, which is "our being, our existence, our be, our WE ARE," which is the plural of I AM. Looking at the meaning of these three Greek words sure magnifies a simple statement and gives it way more depth. The ultimate objective of I AM is to live out our destiny from God with Him as our source of life, our source for every movement, and our source of existence. Like God saying, "I AM the God of Abraham, the God of Isaac and the God of Jacob. God is not the God of the dead but of the living" (Matthew 22:32). You can only fulfill your I AM while you are here on earth alive and empowered with the capacity to do so; destiny is for the living, moving being.

OBJECTIVE WITH PURPOSE

An objective which can be interpreted to be a goal can also be interpreted as an end, the final destination. The Greek word *telos* means "the limit at which a thing ceases to be, termination, the last in any succession or series, eternal, that by which a thing is finished, the end to which all things relate, the aim, or the purpose." There is much talk about purpose in recent times, and rightly so as we seem to have a generation of people without any aim, goal, or objective in life. Few seem to think there is a *telos* in life, a limit at which a thing ceases to be, a time where I AM will either have been accomplished or will not. We only have one shot at accomplishing I AM; none of us really want to get to the end without our I AM objective having been fulfilled. None of us want to live what could have been, should have been, or would have been. We all want to be I AM; we all want to accomplish I AM. We all can accomplish I AM, but you must set I AM as your objective and think it, speak it, and live it. I AM is yours, but you must endure to the *telos*/ end.

Jesus understood His objective long before He accomplished it, long before He got to His statement, "It is finished." He said the things concerning Me have an end. His "I AM" statements were all strategically designed and implemented by Him to bring Him to His objective.

God in His wisdom set things in position and in motion for objectives to be accomplished; it is unfortunate that we sometimes get caught in the process rather than accomplishing the objective. In writing to the Ephesians, Paul told them that God had given some to be apostles, prophets, evangelists, pastors, and teachers. While we have had and still have many people functioning in these offices, many have found rest in the position rather than striving to complete the objective. Paul, however, does lay out very carefully the objective to be accomplished by the operation of these individuals. The objectives are to equip the saints for the work of ministry so that the body of Christ is built up to a place of unity in the faith, in the knowledge of the Son of God and a place of perfection, stature, and the fullness of Christ. God's objective for all of this is for maturity, that His children will no longer be tossed to and fro and carried about with every wind of doctrine from tricky, cunning, crafty, deceitful, and plotting men (See Ephesians 4:11-14).

There is objective in I AM just as there is objective in everything that God has ordained and ordered. It has long disturbed me that the offices mentioned above are always of the ministers doing all the "ministry" and ministering to the very "saints" over and over again. The objectives never seem to be accomplished as the body of Christ is built numerically but not necessarily to a place of fullness of Christ.

FAITH

There is a dimension of faith that is "the faith" to which unity is an objective and in the context of understanding I AM and fulfilling I AM. This I already mentioned in chapter one, taken from John 17 and 2 Corinthians 13:5 and regarding oneness and fullness of Christ in our lives.

We in turn are told by the writer of the book of Hebrews in 3:14, "We have become partakers of Christ if we hold the beginning of our confidence firmly to the end." We too have an end we must be working towards, an end that has had a beginning, an end that has principles for accomplishing, and an end that has an objective to

~ The Objectives of "I AM" ~

arrive at. The end we are working towards is totally dependent on us applying the "I AM" objective.

Peter, writing his first letter in the first chapter, verses 8 and 9, lays out a first principle we must know. He writes concerning the revelation of Jesus Christ, "Whom having not seen you love. Though now you do not see Him you believe, you rejoice with joy inexpressible and full of glory, receiving the (*telos*) end of your faith, the salvation of your souls." Folks, the objective of the "I AM" principle is to bring your faith to a place of completion, an end, its "I AM" objective which is ultimately the salvation of your life.

Many view salvation as a principle for some religious practice or some particular religious ideology and unfortunately miss the point that we all need to be saved.

The objective of putting faith in anything is that it can "save" you, yes, even the chair you just put your faith in and sat in saved you from hitting the ground. While hitting the ground might hurt only slightly, it can also have severe long-lasting effects on your life. The effects of not applying I AM to your life can bring your objective or lack thereof to a deadly conclusion. I AM has as its objective taking you to your personal, fulfilled, final destiny, goal, or end.

Step out in faith, be bold and declare who you are now as though you are already there, pull the future into your present now, and live your I AM, yes you can.

You would think Jesus knew something about objective; He concluded His ministry by saying, "I AM Alpha and Omega, the Beginning and the End, the First and the Last" and "I AM the root and the offspring of David, the bright and morning star" (Revelation 22:13 and 16).

SIN SYNDROME

Like everything else in life, there are viruses, diseases, situations, and circumstances that can hinder your progress if you allow them to do so. The mingled seed syndrome is the one deadly virus that can destroy the "I AM" principle and consequently the "I AM" objective. This begins by God saying in Leviticus 19:19, "You shall not sow your field with mingled/mixed seed." The principle concludes with, "Do not be deceived God is not mocked, for whatever a man sows that he will also reap" (Galatians 6:7). In between these sayings, teachings, and declarations, we have the following in Ezra 9:2: "They have taken some of their daughters as wives for themselves and their sons, so that the holy seed is mingled/mixed with the peoples of those lands. Indeed the hands of the leaders and rulers has been foremost in this sin." Please note that the word used for "mingled" or "mixed" here is the Hebrew word *Arab*. Then there is in Ecclesiastes 3:1-8, "To everything there is a season, a time for every purpose under heaven…a time to sow and a time to reap." Then Jesus, the "I AM," teaches in Luke 8 a parable about a sower who went out to sow and in His explanation He says the seed is the word of God. Then the apostle Paul, another who understands I AM, says to the Romans in 10:17, "Faith comes by hearing, and hearing by the word of God."

The conclusion to the mingled/mixed seed syndrome in the context of releasing the "I AM" principle and objective is that "I AM" words spoken must be pure and continuous, not mixed with any "I AM" that is not in keeping with one's God-given purpose and destiny. The more you speak the "I AM" that is in keeping with who you truly are, the more you will hear it and the more it will yield an "I AM" harvest in your life. Faith in God comes by hearing the word of God, and your confidence and self-assurance will come from hearing your words, the same principle.

This could quite likely be the one straw that breaks the camel's back with regard to the maturing and ultimate fulfillment of the saints of God. Paul had as his major objective the maturity of the children of God and said, "My little children for whom I labour in birth again until Christ is formed in you" (Galatians 4:19). Paul knew and applied the "I AM" principle in his own life; he knew he learnt the principle from the Christ whom he followed, and therefore Paul wanted everyone to grow to that place of maturity.

~ The Objectives of "I AM" ~

Observation has shown me that while much is spoken and sung that is positive and in keeping with God's word, the release of truth and the revelation that the church must be built on is lacking in constants and continuity. There is much mingled/mixed seed being sown into our lives that consequently produce a mingled/mixed faith. Just maybe this is the answer to the double-mindedness that is so common and the unstableness that is so prevalent. We sing songs that are irrelevant to our present situation, we make petitions for situations already dealt with, we ask for things we already have, and we speak with anticipation rather than from a perspective of accomplishment. We can change that.

ACCOMPLISHMENT

If it is finished then it is finished, and the rest of God must become evident in our words and all of our lives. We are either living a life expecting and anticipating God to do something for us or living one that is in keeping with the accomplishments and declarations of our Lord Jesus Christ. Look at the role of the church with regard to accomplishment in Ephesians 3:10-11: "to the intent that now the manifold wisdom of God must be made known by the church to the principalities and powers in the heavenly places, according to the eternal purpose which He accomplished in Christ Jesus our Lord." The bottom line is we mingle/mix our seeds constantly between the right and the not-right and expect to reap a particular harvest. Truth be told, our individual fields are inundated with weeds from unholy seeds planted alongside the holy ones. We have constantly and continually mixed holy seed with unholy seed, so how can we possibly expect a holy crop?

An objective must be our first priority: in the same way businesses set strategic measures to accomplish their goals and objectives, so too should we as believers. Of course, we have to know our objectives in order to set any measure of strategy for accomplishing. If we know the criterion set by God for those for whom Christ will return to receive, I would think that's an excellent starting point. We are constantly told that Christ's coming again is for a "glorious church" again; we are told His bride will be "without spot or wrinkle." I would conclude then that our objective as a church and bride would be to iron out any wrinkles, scrub out all spots, and prepare ourselves to be in a glorious condition for His return. After all, it does say in Revelation 19:7, "the marriage of the Lamb has come and His wife/bride has made herself ready." Are we making ourselves ready? Are we as His bride preparing ourselves to be radiant and absolutely stunning and beautiful for Him, the groom?

Is that our primary objective in life?
Can you and I honestly say, " I AM doing that?"

See how Paul tells the Ephesians about this expectation: "Husbands love your wife, just as Christ also loved the church and gave Himself for her, that He might sanctify and cleanse her with the washing of water by the word, that He will present her to Himself a glorious church not having spot or wrinkle or any such thing, but that she will be holy and without blemish" (Ephesians 5:25-27). The word of God has the power to wash you, cleanse you, and prepare you; the word of "I AM" has the potential to take you to your destiny. You can accomplish your objectives.

The time to plant is over, every seed has been sown, Jesus Christ has fulfilled all the requirements necessary for us to live our I AM as He lived His I AM, He has met all criterion, and it is our time to reap.

Let me make the "I AM" objective simple for you using a piece of Paul's letter to the Colossians; you can read it yourself in Colossians 1:27-29.

1. When <u>Christ is IN you</u>, there is hope of glory.

2. When <u>you are IN Christ</u>, you will be perfected.

3. The objective is only accomplished through <u>His working IN you.</u>

I AMness is an "IN" thing that leads to an "I can, yes you can."

Chapter Three
The "I AM" That Is God

<u>THE BEST LESSONS ON I AM
ARE FROM THE GREAT I AM.</u>

"I AM who I AM."

<u>"GOD"</u>

Let us begin this chapter by applying some common sense to the word *god* and its meaning. Most dictionaries will tell you the word *god* means things like "superior being, creator, ruler of the universe, moral authority, superhuman being or spirit, eternal and immortal, etc." One thing that is represented by all of the above names is certainly superiority, and therefore we can conclude that god/God is in a superior position to natural or mortal man. From this perspective then, let us look at the "God" of the Bible and see if this "God" lives up to the title or definitions given for the position.

What about a God who says test and prove Me and see if I AM who I say I AM? Or Jesus asking if anyone can accuse Him of any sin. Sounds pretty Godlike to me to be bold enough to make such statements.

~ I AM therefore I CAN ~

You be the judge; you try God and see if He is real; you see if this "I AM" I speak of is of any real substance.

<u>I AM, I BE</u>

When asked a question to which one will usually respond with an "I AM," that question is quite likely to be a present tense question. "Are you Brent?" "I AM," providing that you are, of course. "Are you the mechanic?" "I AM," if that is your vocation and for which you are known and/or often identified. Many such questions can be asked of you with reference to who you are; with the ones they get right, of course, your answer will have to be "I AM," because you are.

When Moses was confronted by God, Moses asked God not an "are you" question, but Moses asked God to tell him His name. Moses needed at that moment to know God's name so he would have an answer for those who might ask what is God's name, a reasonable question when you do not know the answer and need one.

God replied to Moses, "I AM WHO I AM." Or "WHO I AM IS I AM" (Exodus 3:14).

There are some who maintain that the proper translation from Hebrew for the words *ehyeh asher ehyeh* is "I shall be that I shall be." Others say it should literally be "I be that I be." When I look at the passage of the same text written in Hebrew, I see only two identical Hebrew words following each other, which are *ehyeh ehyeh*, which in English is translated "to be." So God being a person and therefore personalizing it said, "I BE I BE," or just maybe the proper translation should have been "I AM I AM."

This word in Hebrew that is translated "I BE" or "I AM" comes from the same word for YHWH (pronounced "Yahweh") and which is rendered in English as Jehovah and literally means "The Existing One." Well I do not profess to be any expert on Hebrew at all, so I am not the one to say what is correct. However, what is certain given all the different versions of what was said is the word BE, which is first person singular present and therefore is equivalent to I AM. So, if someone is saying, "I shall be that I shall be," "I AM I AM," or "I be that I be," or just simply, "I be I be," it tells me they have the capacity to be that which they need to be.

THE NAMES

Actually, when I think about it I can see God operating like that because He was whatever He had to be in any given situation. He was Jehovah the provider as Jireh, Jehovah the healer as Ropheka, Jehovah of peace as Shalom, Jehovah the shepherd as Rohi, Jehovah the maker as Hoseenu, and many, many others. In His capacity as Jehovah God He can be "I shall," He can be "I be," or He can be "I AM." His attributes speak louder for Him than any name can. Let's face it: He can be called Jehovah and that is His name, but when Jireh follows Jehovah, then it makes it more powerful and meaningful. He becomes the God that provides. So the adding of Jireh is what puts the "be" to what He is "being" at the time of providing. With all the number of names that God was known as, they were named after all the individual attributes He was as He delivered or produced. Same individual, same God, same Jehovah, same person, but He became I AM Jehovah Ropheka when healing was needed and healing He delivered.

Can we really ever understand the awesomeness of the "I BE," the "I AM"? Can we comprehend the essence of not living limited by time? Can we fathom the past, the present, and the future as one dimension without any borders? Can we see all time as the now?

While God speaking to Moses and revealing His name was the first time God used the I AM, it certainly was not the last. The context of God telling Moses His name was to ensure that Moses knew the awesome capacity of the I AM and that He, God, was using him only as the human element to deliver the people of Israel out of Egypt. Hundreds of times after this encounter God continually says, "I AM the God who delivered you out of Egypt. I AM the God who brought you out of bondage in Egypt. I AM the God who delivered you from slavery in Egypt." While Moses was the person being seen, the person up front, the man present and doing what had to be done to mobilize the movement of Israel out of Egypt, was the God I AM at work. I AM in its essence therefore is at the root of all deliverance and salvation, all emancipation and freedom. "I AM" can.

QUESTIONS, QUESTIONS

Is it only God that can live the I AM?

This is the number one question before us. While there may be many others questions and there definitely should be, the paramount question is, is it only God that can live the I AM? Is I AM limited to the great I AM? Is He unique in I AMness or has He passed on His abilities or principles to anyone or ones?

When God said "Let Us make man in our image and likeness," and consequently did so (Genesis 1:26-27), did He include His I AMness in man's DNA? Did God download any I AM into anyone? Is I AM transferable?

The above are very viable questions, and we should seek answers. The God I AM said to man at the point of original creation to have dominion, subdue, and rule. Please note that when I speak of man here I am not talking of male man only. When God spoke the words of dominion and rule there was no person yet created; He therefore was speaking of His intentions and plans for mankind. When He actually created the original man in His image and His likeness, He created him a completed being, male and female, blessed them both, and said to them both, "Be fruitful and multiply, fill the earth and subdue it, have dominion…" (Genesis 1:28). Later on, God formed man and he became a living being, and a little later on God then made the woman from the man, or took the woman out of the man, or separated the male man from the wo(mb)man and she also became a living being. Now the man had a mate to help him, to support him, one with a womb and therefore capable of re-creating, multiplying, or replenishing, a mate taken from inside of him now outside of him to be with him.

TRANSFERENCE

Then there is another situation when God sees mankind collaborating and planning in unity to build the Tower of Babel (Genesis 11:1-6), and He says nothing they (plural I AM) propose to do will be withheld from them. It sure looks like man has some potential for greatness; of course, when this potential is used abnormally or for abnormal use (i.e., abused), then God gets concerned.

Then David writing in Psalm 8:3-6 says, "When I consider the heavens, the works of your hands, the moon and the stars which you have ordained. What is man that you are mindful of him, and the son of man that you visit him? You have made him a little lower than Elohim and You have crowned him with glory and honor. You have made him to have dominion over the works of your hands, You have put all things under his feet." In other words, this great creating God who has put in place all the universe and set it in order, this great I AM God is thinking about man. First God made man only a little lower than Himself (Elohim), then He crowned him and gave him rule over everything. I would say I AM is, if not natural to the DNA of man, at least transferable at the point of connectivity to the great I AM.

It is my opinion that God is not alone as I AM; He is not selfish and exclusively controlling I AMness. He is the source and originator of I AM, but anyone connected to Him can live I AM. I AM is available to every son of God and, I might boldly add, available to some degree to anyone brave enough to apply the principles. After all, a principle is just that, a principle, and therefore if applied, it will produce. It's like a seed: one does not have to be a farmer or gardener to get results; apply the principles of sowing and reap the harvest. As the principle of giving is not limited to any particular group, apply the principle, be a blessing, and be blessed. Apply the principles of God, speak I AM to your situations, and see them change. Yes, you can.

I AMness has its roots in God; I AMness found fulfillment in Jesus Christ; I AMness is one of the most powerful biblical principles there is. Everything that you would like to be and you are not, you can; it is found in I AMness. Everything you hope to achieve will be more easily attained with the principle of I AMness. All your "I can" comes right after your "I AM."

FUTURE TALK

"I AM CALLS THINGS THAT ARE NOT NOW AS THOUGH THEY ARE NOW" (Romans 4:17).

God as the great I AM speaks to every situation as being in the future. He calls everyone according to their destiny and He sees and calls everyone as the finished, completed persons that they are. God sent an angel to visit a man called Gideon in Judges 6:11-12. Gideon was threshing wheat in a wine press because of the oppression of the Midianites. Gideon was an ordinary dude with no military might or expertise, but God referred to him as a mighty man of strength, no doubt Gideon looked over his shoulder to see who was being addressed. God called Gideon not according to his present position of weakness but from his future position of strength, success, and accomplishments.

God had David anointed as King of Israel and even with Saul still on the throne, He constantly spoke to David as though he was already the king. Your present position is certainly not your final destination. Every successful motivational speaker, godly or ungodly, has tapped into the successful principles of I AMness. One calls it the giant that needs to be awakened within you, another relates it to stinking thinking, one calls it realizing your potential, whatever the terminology used, the principle remains the same. I AMness is the answer to your future hopes, dreams, and desires. I AMness can cause you to say "I can."

GODNESS

Given the operation of this God that I call the great I AM and how He operates and functions to provide and protect people, to win wars against enemies, one who always has the best interest of people at the fore, one who allows for the miraculous and supernatural to be accomplished on earth, does this God live up to the expectations of a "God"?

God the creator of everything, God who was before everything that there is, God who is capable of any and everything, God who is rightly referred to as Almighty, is truly ALL mighty, this God is the great I AM. You need to get connected to this great God, not the god of religion, not the god of organizations, not a god limited to a building or a time and place, but to the great God who is the great I AM. When you get connected and tuned in to His vibes, then the I AM that He is becomes the I AM that you can be.

I am well aware that the very word "God" immediately conjures thoughts of religion, and then of course is associated with your perception developed from your associations. However, this is not about what you think it is; this is not about going to any building, or doing or not doing any list of rules and regulations. This is about a one-on-one relationship with a superior person who is capable of turning your natural into the supernatural; this is a spiritual connection with I AM. This is a one-on-one father-son relationship that is continually empowered by close fellowship.

TWOGETHERNESS

The I AM that I AM talking about is about you networking with the I AM that has the potential to fulfill you completely and the capacity to deliver you to your destiny.

I AM is about one-on-one with I AM. This is being brought to a place of complete unity, this is being intrinsically woven "TWOgether" with God, this is in keeping with the words spoken by Jesus Christ. He begins His discourse in the 14th chapter of John, verse 20, "At that day you will know that I AM IN My Father and you IN Me and Me IN you." He continues in chapter 15:2-7, "Every branch IN Me that does not bear fruit He takes away, and every branch that bears fruit He prunes, that it bears more fruit. You are already clean because of the word which I have spoken to you. Abide IN Me and I IN you, as the branch cannot bear fruit of itself, unless it abides IN the vine, neither can you unless you abide IN Me. I am the vine you are the branches. He who abides IN Me and I IN him, bears much fruit; for without Me you can do nothing. If anyone does not abide IN Me he is cast out as a branch and is withered and they gather them and throw them in the fire and they are burned. If you abide IN Me and My words abide in you, you will ask what you desire and it shall be done for you." In John 16:33 Jesus says, "IN Me you will have peace." Then He concludes in chapter 17, "that they all be one as you Father are IN Me and I IN You, that they also be one IN us, that the world will believe that You sent Me, and the glory which You gave Me, I have given them, that they be one just as We are one. I IN them and you IN Me that they be made perfect in one and that the world will know that You have sent Me, and have loved them as You have loved Me" (John 17:21-23). In the closing chapters of life in the flesh here on earth, Jesus is praying for His disciples and those who would believe through their message. His entire trust is oneness, completeness in unity, being woven together; it's a passage pregnant with the desires of one who knows the Father's heart.

To be created in an image is to image that from which one is created, to image God the creator, the great I AM, is our primary purpose on this earth. Everything else in life falls below this in the list of priorities. Like Paul tells the Philippians in 4:13, "I can do all things through Christ who gives me strength." When you are IN Him, then everything is from Him and everything is through Him. All your "I cans" are possible, yes you can.

The best lessons on I AM are from the great I AM. I challenge you to learn the lessons of I AM from I AM, pass the tests presented by I AM, and fulfill your own I AM to the max. I AM has the potential to make you into the I AM you were destined to be. I AM has the capacity to transform your life to being the secure, confident, successful, caring person you are meant to be.

I AM is It.

~ The "I AM" That Is God ~

Understand I AM, embrace I AM, implement and practice I AM. I AM confident you will never regret releasing your I AM and becoming the person you are destined to be.

In its simplest form, I AMness is summed up in Ephesians 5:1: *"BE imitators of God as dearly loved children."* You can read it in context from Ephesians 4:25-5:7.

Chapter Four
SONSHIP and I AM

<u>Sonship is the ultimate fulfillment
of the essence of the Father.</u>

"You have received the Spirit of sonship."

HEIRS TO INHERITANCE

Quite possibly the most powerful, motivating, and encouraging spiritual principle universally is that of "sonship." When one understands the dynamics of sonship and applies the principle of sonship, there is no stopping that person.

Son is a legal term and not a biological term, so ladies please take no offense, you are a son of God as I as a man am the bride of Christ.

Sonship is a vital piece of wisdom that must be understood in the context of transference from the old to the new. The most important concept that was changed by Jesus Christ was of God being a Father rather than a "God." What I mean by this is that God became more personal and more intimate. The first two words in the teaching on prayer by Jesus is "Our Father." We must understand that a transference took place from old to new; while principles remained the same, methods changed. Prayer took on a more personal one-on-one with the introduction to "Our Father," that is the essence of sonship.

We have already seen in chapter one that I AMness is really about oneness with the great I AM, and I AM can only be fully realized when one is connected or linked to the great I AM. The only true oneness connection or link to the great I AM must be in sonship. Sonship is the ultimate fulfillment of the essence of the great I AM being lived out by a son. When one says what his father says and does what his father does, then sonship is being manifest and made visible.

In the Hebrew mind, sonship is totally associated with a oneness between father and son. The son has his own personal name and uses the father's first name as his surname. David son of Jesse or David ben Jesse. Now we can understand why the Jews wanted to stone Jesus for claiming oneness with God, as The Son of God.

The word *sonship* must be understood because it is not always used as such. While the word *son* in its singular and plural form appears over 3000 times in the Bible (it must be an important concept), *sonship* appears very few times and is also translated "adoption." The Greek word *huiothesia* is from two Greek words: *huio*, which is "son," and *thesia* from the root *tithemi*, which means "to place." Consequently the word for adoption or sonship really literally means "son-place" or more accurately, "to be placed as a son."

"I AM GIVES A SON THE POWER TO BE WHAT THE FATHER IS."

When I read Matthew 18:11 ff. in context, as all scripture should be read, it could very well be that Jesus is referring to "that which was lost" as the saving or restoration of sonship. Be mindful that the context of the scripture ensures that one is already a sheep and part of the flock. However, there is a separation from the others, and therefore the restoration is one of fellowship and not relationship.

~ SONSHIP and I AM ~

The lesson from the beginning is about children, which He calls little ones further on and warns of not despising. After all, Paul tells us in Ephesians 1:5 that sonship/adoption is what we were predestined for.

REPENTANCE AND COVENANT

Regarding the spiritual principle of sonship, Paul writes to the Romans in chapter 8:11-17, "If the Spirit of Him who raised Jesus from the dead dwells IN you, He who raised Christ from the dead will also give life to your mortal bodies, through His Spirit who dwells IN you. Therefore, brothers we are debtors not to the flesh to live according to it. For if you live according to the flesh you will die, but if by the Spirit you put to death the deeds of the flesh you will live. For as many as are led by the Spirit of God are sons of God. For you did not again receive the spirit of bondage and fear, but you received the Spirit of adoption by whom we cry out, 'Abba, Father.' The Spirit Himself bears witness with our spirit that we are children/sons of God, and if sons then heirs, heirs of God and coheirs with Christ if we suffer with Him that we also be glorified together." Paul teaches them on this dynamic formula for their release. He first makes it very clear that there are two sides to every person, the flesh, or natural side and the spiritual one. He concludes by determining that the natural side cannot please God and therefore in order to please God, one must be in the spirit, and this is possible only when the Spirit of God dwells IN you. In the context of our subject matter, sonship then equals I AM and is only possible if the original great I AM is the empowerment of your individual I AM. Paul also says that the only way to put to death or destroy the workings of the natural and bring release from destruction and death is by the Spirit. In other words, as Paul summarizes the principle, he is convinced that "as many as are led by the Spirit of God these are sons of God." And again, "you received the Spirit of sonship by whom we cry out, 'Abba, Father'."

I think of sonship in the context of repentance; there is much talk of repentance in the Bible and rightly so, for it is necessary for turning to the Father and thus reconciling with the Father. However, there is a dimension of repentance that I have observed which is also necessary for continued fellowship with the Father as a son. The word *repentance*, like most *re*-words, speaks of something being redone since the *re* means "again." *Pent* is a derivative of the word *penned*, meaning "to be enclosed or confined." So the concept of repentance that I refer to is in being again penned up with or enclosed with the Father, an intimacy in fellowship that goes beyond relationship and your average closeness.

In the same way, *covenant* is a word and concept that is widely used in the Bible from the beginning of time to now. *Covenant* also is a word that means or represents a joining "two-gether"; *covenant* literally means, "to fetter" or "to chain together." The Father is constantly looking for sons; He is continually looking for sonship to be manifested on the earth. Like the father of the prodigal sons searching the horizon for a son coming home, so too our heavenly Father is anxiously awaiting you to come home and fulfill your I AM.

RELATIONSHIP AND FELLOWSHIP

Let me say at this point that I make a clear distinction between relationship and fellowship, relationship being a one-time completed concept of connection in whatever realm, fellowship being the continuity of the given relationship. For example, I can have a relationship as father to many children for that is how we are related, and similarly for a husband and wife. However, our being related or being in a relationship is no guarantee of continued fellowship, which is subject to the parties doing. So, my relationship with Father God, the great I AM, is that of a son; my fellowship is that which will determine how closely linked we are and in turn what I learn from my Father and then how well I image my Father.

Sonship then is the very essence of I AMness; I AM can only find true possible release through sonship.

In order to understand the great potential that this sonship has in life,

~ SONSHIP and I AM ~

the apostle Paul tells the Romans in 8:18 ff. that all of creation is expectantly awaiting the manifestation of sonship. I want to be sure you get this: creation, which means all that has been created, all of this creation is eagerly awaiting people here on planet earth to live out and make visible their individual sonship/I AM of the Father to which they belong.

This creation is in bondage, this creation is suffering, this creation is frustrated, this creation is corrupt and can only be set free by the release of sonship. This creation longs to share in the freedom, the liberty, and the emancipation that sonship enjoys. Sonship or I AMness is the key to the release of all that is heavenly, all that is spiritual, all that is from the source, all that is God.

Paul writing to the Galatians from 3:26-4:7 tells them about their sonship, their oneness, and their promise, that once they were children in bondage under the elements of the world (creation and its corruption) but now the fullness of time has come. In other words, that is what you were, but now a new season, a new dispensation, a new release is come to you. This is a season of maturity, this is the season of the release of sonship, this is the season for now. We have been children and childish for too long; we were under guardians and stewards being protected and trained, we had laws and commandments, but now the appointed time has come. Look at Paul's words: "when the fullness of the time had come, God sent forth His Son, born of a woman, born under law to redeem those who were under the law that we might receive the full rights of sons and because you are now a son God sent the Spirit of His Son into your hearts, crying out, 'Abba, Father.' Therefore, you are no longer a slave but a son, and if a son, then an heir of God through Christ." We are positioned on this earth for this time of release; it is the time to think, talk, and walk like an heir to the throne of God. It is time to manifest sonship on this earth; it is the precise and accurate time now to be "I AM" to the world. Yes, you can.

There is a definite turning point from slavery to sonship, and there is a season of fulfillment to all who would embrace it. True emancipation is realized only through sonship and the manifestation of same. Paul confirms this truth when he writes to the Ephesians in 1:4-5 and tells them that God predestined them to sonship under His Fatherhood according to the good pleasure of His will. From the opening days after creation, God always makes a distinction between the sons of God and those of men; He always purposed to have sons that would live out His characteristics, His personality, and His nature. This is imaging, the purpose for which we were created.

IMAGING/SPIRITUAL SONSHIP

This is awesome business, folks: God the Almighty creator who spoke everything into being and sustains everything by His great power, this great and mighty God puts time and effort into adoption, to bring sons into His family. The ultimate purpose of man is to image God on this earth, reflecting Him, representing Him, and shadowing Him, which are all modes of showing His image and likeness.

Sons and sonship is a theme throughout history, more so God's history, or is it "His-story"? We have a history of righteousness and unrighteousness paralleled and recorded in the dynamics of the two births necessary for man to become sons of God, the birth of flesh and the birth of spirit. Early in history, Genesis 6 gives us a picture of sons of God and daughters of men that equates the dimension of the natural and supernatural, or the flesh and spirit.

Cain and Abel were the first sons of Adam and Eve, then there is a lot said about Isaac and Ishmael, the sons of Abraham; then there is Jacob and Esau, the sons of Isaac; the twelve tribes of Israel came from twelve sons of Jacob, whose name was changed to Israel. Then there were Jesse's sons and David one of them, rising to become the jewel king of Israel, followed by his son Solomon and on and on. God also referred to the nation of Israel as His firstborn son and commanded Pharaoh to let His son go or He will kill his firstborn sons. God in His wisdom always works with the principle of sowing and reaping, and sons are always referred to as seed. Early up after Adam and Eve messed up and God was pronouncing curses for their

~ SONSHIP and I AM ~

action, He promised the serpent that there will be enmity between his seed and the woman's seed (Genesis 3:15).

Sonship has always been foundational in God's plans for representation, restoration, and redemption.

Sons of light, sons of God, sons of the resurrection, all terms of reference for the realm of sonship. John tells us that as many as receive Jesus, He gave them the right to become children/sons of God (John 1:12). Of course, like everything else there is a flip side to it as well, and those not receiving Christ and hence manifesting a different character are called sons of disobedience and sons of the devil (John 8:44).

Arriving at an indication of the meaning of sonship within the culture of biblical times is vitally important. In this culture, it was assumed that a son would be what his father was and therefore train under his father and eventually enter into the same vocation. If his father was a tentmaker, it was assumed the son would be a tentmaker as well. If the father was a farmer, then a son would almost always be a farmer. If the father was a carpenter, then a son would be expected to be a carpenter as well, following in his father's steps. So, "like father like son" was a cultural norm. This reminds me of Jesus' statement when He says, "blessed are the peacemakers for they shall be called sons of God" (Matthew 5:9). He is saying that peacemaking is a like a vocation to God the Father, and those who follow after God in that respect can be considered sons of God. Like Father, like son. I can do what Father does.

Similarly, when we read of Barnabas, the son of encouragement, we can see that the assumption behind the term is that Barnabas is all about encouragement, and that his father must necessarily have been the very embodiment of encouragement. Thus, Barnabas is the equal to his father. When Jesus indicates that He is doing the work of His father, it is an implicit claim to equality with the Father. He is claiming to be God's Son in a way that far transcends a human relationship to God. The Jews understood the deeper meaning of Jesus' words and were infuriated to the point of gathering stones to throw at Him, claiming that Jesus had committed blasphemy.

Sonship is in fact a representation by a son of the attributes and skills of the father. When I was young we had a saying, "monkey see, monkey do," and of course it's not about monkeying around but about mimicking the father that you admired.

Here is the principle of sonship as written to the Hebrews: "God who at various times and in various ways spoke in time past to the fathers by the prophets, has in these last days spoken to us by His Son, whom He has appointed heir of all things, through whom also He made the worlds; who being the brightness of His glory and the express image of His person and upholding all things by the word of His power, when He had by Himself purged our sins, sat down at the right hand of the Majesty on high, having become so much better than the angels as He has by inheritance obtained a more excellent name than they, for to which of the angels did He ever say, 'You are My Son'..." (Hebrews 1:1-5).

Sonship is being a representation of the nature and character of the father. Sonship is being like the ambassador for the father, and it is presented to the Hebrews who followed God but did not understand the principle and power of sonship. This is made clear by Jesus' words in John 8:38-39: "I speak what I have seen with My Father, and you do what you have seen with your father." They answered and said to Him, "Abraham is our father." Jesus said to them, "If you were Abraham's children you would do the works of Abraham." A little further on He told them that their actions of attempting to kill Him was a representation of their real father. So the bottom line is our words and actions are a clear indication of who our father is, whom we represent and image.

God had originally planned the principle of sonship and hence imaging to be fulfilled by His creation of the man Adam. When Adam did not fulfill his purpose as a son, God then decided to implement through Jacob/Israel the representation He desired on earth. Unfortunately, Israel as a nation missed the concept as well and never fulfilled the sonship role either. Because of this, God had to finally send His only Son to get the message across and the mandate accomplished, hence the writer to the Hebrews pointing out so very clearly the principle of sonship:

> "Children have never been very good
> at listening to their elders,
> but they have never failed to imitate them."

NATURAL SONSHIP

Probably the best natural example of sonship training is the molding and shaping of a prince in an earthly kingdom to be one day the king. Many in the western world are familiar with Prince Charles and his grooming to be one day King of England. His training began from birth and continues throughout his life. He is over 60 years old, and he is still waiting for his opportunity to exercise all that he has learnt and is learning in preparation to be king. However, while he awaits his turn to be the king and monarch of his country, he continually functions and represents as a son the leadership of his parents and their kingdom. Much of his training is formal and structured with deliberate and precise modes and methods with specific goals. However, a great deal of his learning and hands-on experiences and training will be derived from him observing his father and mother as they function in their capacity as monarchs. The same is true in every other kingdom: Monaco, Holland, Sweden, Japan, and the Arabian kingdoms.

Many times in life our best training comes from practical, personal involvement with those who have already accomplished.

Someone said of Niccolo Machiavelli's book *The Prince*, "Here is the world's most famous master plan for seizing and holding power." Take this statement as you like, take it or leave it, but the principle is true. The best plan for seizing and holding power for your life is in sonship to the King of the universe, the great I AM, embracing and patterning the great I AM and releasing the I AM that you are born to be.

~ I AM therefore I CAN ~

Sonship is about resemblance, reflection, and representation of a father; sonship is simply the role of imaging a father. I can be like father. Sonship is the ultimate fulfillment of the essence of the father.

Sonship is quite simply summed up as intimacy with Father.

Chapter Five
JESUS, the "I AM"

IN BECOMING ANYTHING IN LIFE, ONE MUST HAVE A MENTOR.

> "Most assuredly I say to you,
> before Abraham was, I AM."

THE ULTIMATE MENTOR

Jesus Christ spoke similar words to the words that God spoke. John writes that Jesus said, "Most assuredly I say to you, before Abraham was, I AM" (John 8:58). His hearers picked up stones to throw at Him because they understood that He was equating Himself to God because Abraham was thousands of years before Jesus. After all, who else can live without the limitations of time frames? Who but God can live past, present, and future as one time zone?

Actually in that very chapter eight of John's gospel, Jesus sets the stage for His "I AM" declaration that nearly got Him stoned, long before He actually declared it. He began by dealing with the scene of the woman caught (without mention of any man) in adultery by not condemning her but rather charging her to go and sin no more (John

8:11). Not an average statement made by any ordinary one. He then says in verse 12, "I AM the light of the world, he who follows Me shall not walk in darkness, but have the light of life." Hmmm, strange fellow! He then says in verse 14, "I know where I AM from and where I AM going." This is something I pray and hope that many will know, for it will set the stage for potential realized. He continues and says in verse 16, "I AM not alone but I AM with the Father who sent Me." He does not stop His discourse but continues in verse 18, "I AM One who bears witness of Myself and the Father who sent Me bears witness of Me." You would think they would get the picture of who He was by then, or at least grasp what He was saying. Knowing they did not get it, Jesus continues in verse 21-23, "I AM going away and you will seek Me and you will die in your sin. Where I go you cannot come ... You are from beneath I AM from above, you are of this world; I AM not of this world." He concludes this portion by saying in verse 24, "If you do not believe that I AM He you will die in your sins." And verse 28: "When you lift up the Son of Man then you will know that I AM He."

Now tell me, this has to be a madman or a very sane man who understands the power of I AM. The truth is, they did not pick up stones just based on His final I AM statement concerning Abraham, but from a culmination of all the "I AM" declarations prior to this.

In an Old Testament context, God reveals Himself by many different names as we saw earlier. God's names always represented the particular attribute or characteristic for which He was then living out. In the New Testament, these same attributes and characteristics were lived out in the person of Jesus Christ, one person, one name. He healed, He provided, He is Peace, He is the great shepherd, and everything that God was and is, that's what gave Jesus the right to say, before Abraham was, I AM. The Jews, hearing this statement from Him, knew exactly what it meant, what He meant. Jesus Christ is the manifestation of God on the earth, hence the remark that He will be called Emmanuel, God with us.

~ JESUS, the "I AM" ~

THE CLAIMS

Is it only the man Jesus that can live the I AM, or is it a principle that can be lived by anyone bold and brave enough to go for it? That is the big question I hope we can answer here. Of course, we must keep all this in context with the very words of Jesus. He said in John 5:30, "I can do nothing on my own, as I hear I judge and My judgment is righteous because I do not seek My own will but the will of the Father who sent Me." The "I AM" and "I can" claims of Jesus are always in keeping with connectivity with the great I AM.

Since we know when Jesus Christ made His I AM statement, the result was a mob on his heels. Let us look at His other statements that could help answer our question.

The following is a list of some of the "I AM" statements made by Jesus Christ, most of which were made before He was any of the following. They were absolute statements of faith that He purposed to bring to completion; He knew there would be a day when He would say, "It is finished."

I AM the bread of life.
I AM the light of the world.
I AM from above.
I AM not of this world.
I AM the door.
I AM the Good Shepherd.
I AM gentle and lowly in heart.
I AM the resurrection and the life.
I AM the way, the truth, and the life.
I AM the true vine.
I AM the alpha & the omega.
I AM the first and last.
I AM he that lives, was dead, and I AM alive for evermore.
I AM he that searches hearts.
I AM the root and the offspring of David.
I AM with you always.

Then there are other words Jesus used to say the same thing. Jesus is in conversation with a Samaritan woman in Sychar, teaching her some things which we can all learn even now. He shows no discrimination towards Samaritans, women, or even an adulterous sinful person. He broke the barriers of something that was deep rooted in His Jewish culture and the religion of His people. He continues to speak with her and teaches her the truth about worship, eliminating the temple in Jerusalem, eliminating a mountain in Samaria, or for that matter, any physical place or space as necessary for worship, again breaking the traditional mindset of Jewish tradition and religion. At this point in the conversation the woman says, "I know that Messiah/Christ is coming, when He comes He will tell us all things." Jesus replies, "I who speak to you AM He." In other words, I AM Messiah/Christ (John 4:1-26).

Then a little farther on Jesus says to the Jews, "I and The Father are One" (John 10:30). Well, this resulted in stones being picked up again. Jesus continues His discourse with the Jews nevertheless, teaching them about accusing Him of blasphemy, the difference between God and gods in scripture, and His sanctification and apostleship from the Father. Then He adds, "you say I AM blaspheming because I said, I AM the Son of God?" (John 10:36). Hmmm!

The question begs an answer: is Jesus Christ all that He said or claimed to be in the list above? Was Jesus Christ all the above when He was boldly making those declarations? The answer is that He was NOT at the time of speaking, not at that precise moment of His declarations; He was not all those things that He declared Himself to be. BUT He had every intention of being every one of them in the future. He had every intention of fulfilling the words that He was speaking. Therefore, with that confidence, with that assurance of accomplishing His objectives, He declared them to be as though they already were. He took what was a certain future and pulled it into the present by the words of faith that He uttered. He enacted the "I AM" principle.

Take, for example, while Jesus was still on earth, still here in the world, praying in John 17 at the closing of His ministry. He says, "Now I AM no longer in the world, but these are in the world, and I come to You, Holy Father." While He had not gone anywhere yet, He spoke as though He was already gone to the Father and consequently no longer in the world. His language was always that of purpose and destiny, and His words were always that of future accomplishments and achievements; while being very present in the now, He constantly lived in the future. You can too.

THE CHALLENGES

I fully understand that what I am saying will offend the doctrine of many; the teachings that many hold dearly will be challenged, but please read on. I too hold to the absolute fact that Jesus Christ is Lord. I know there is no other sacrifice for sin than His sinless body from which His blood was shed; I know He died, was buried and was resurrected on the third day and is now seated at the right hand of The Father in heaven. Yes, I am talking about the same Jesus, not another Jesus as Paul warned us some will come preaching. No doubt that Paul knew the real Jesus. Paul was struck down on his way to Damascus by the question, "Why are you persecuting Me?" Paul's response was, "Who are You, Lord?" No doubt Paul knew it was the Lord; what he did not know was who the Lord was, so he got his answer, "I AM Jesus whom you are persecuting..." Paul had his opening encounter with Jesus as the I AM, and he had to fall down (Acts 9:1-5).

This same Jesus was a man like you and I, born of a woman (mankind/female man), born in a very natural normal way like any other male or female man, which is commonly referred to as born of water. This human birth gave Him legal entry into the earth, and consequently He referred to Himself constantly as The Son of Man. Be mindful that He was also born of The Spirit, thus giving Him the equivalence to those of us who have also now had a spiritual rebirth.

On this same Jesus, the writer of Hebrews tells us in 5:8, "although He was a Son, yet He learned obedience by the things which He suffered." Folks, obedience is not something we are born with. Obedience is not a gift. Obedience is something we must learn. Disobedience does come naturally, though. Ever see anyone teaching their children to disobey? Can you imagine my parents saying, "Please, Brenty, can you just disobey just once? Rebel please. Be jealous. Grab a toy away from another child. Tell him 'its mine.' Tell him to 'get away.' " Believe me, they never had to teach Brenty that. No, obedience must be learnt. When people who are opposed to salvation and sin and those who try to justify or minimize their behavior ask, what am I being saved from, why do I need to be saved, etc., they fail to recognize the inherent flow of disobedience in everyone's life. Jesus, with all the wisdom to be debating with folks in the temple at twelve years old, left there and was obedient to His parents from that time on. Learning obedience can be painful, it can be likened unto suffering, it many times feels like you are suffering, but it must be learnt.

THE MAKING PROCESS

The apostle Peter, speaking in the book of Acts 2:36, says, "Let all the house of Israel know assuredly that God has made this Jesus whom you crucified, both Lord and Christ." The book called the Bible could very easily be called "The Making of the Lord Jesus Christ and His Disciples." That reminds me of Jesus saying to His disciples, "follow Me and I will make you fishers of men" (Mark 1:17).

There is a making process we must all go through to arrive at our destiny. God said to Jacob in the book of Genesis, "I AM God, the God of your father, do not fear to go down to Egypt, for I will make of you a great nation there" (Genesis 46:3). There is a making process we must all go through to arrive at our destiny. It might come through years in captivity, and it can very well feel like you are being crucified. Whatever the making process we might undergo, the mindset must always be the fulfilling of the "I AM" in my life.

It is a given fact in every walk of life that once one person accomplishes something, that same once difficult, almost impossible something suddenly becomes doable. There is something about the human psyche that makes following much easier than leading. I guess that's why today we have more followers than leaders, sad but true.

For years, the 4-minute mile was considered not merely unreachable but, according to physiologists of the time, dangerous to the health of any athlete who attempted to reach it. A man called Roger Bannister refused to believe that and decided to be a leader. When he crossed the finish line in 1954 with a time of 3 minutes, 59.4 seconds, he broke through a psychological barrier as well as a physical one. John Landy, considered one of the great milers of that era, had never gotten closer than within 1.5 seconds of the 4-minute barrier before. Within 46 days of Bannister's breakthrough, Landy surpassed the record with a 3:57.9 in Finland. Bannister and Landy raced later in the year in the "Mile of the Century" at Vancouver, a runoff to decide who was the faster miler. Bannister won in 3:58.8 to Landy's 3:59.6, the first time two men in one race had broken 4 minutes. By the end of 1957, 16 runners had logged sub-four-minute miles.

You might or might not be interested in running a fast mile; you might or might not be interested in breaking any records. However, I am sure we all have dreams and aspirations, hopes and desires that we are hoping to accomplish or working towards. This being the case, a lesson from I AM is before us. We too, like all the milers who finally accomplished their dream of a sub-four-minute mile, have someone who has gone before us. Jesus has accomplished through the principle of I AM. Jesus has shown us that our future hopes, dreams, and desires, our every goal and objective, can be realized; we have a chief leader and a finisher of faith. You can do it, yes you can.

THE TESTS

I am always reminded when thinking or teaching on faith, of the words Jesus said to Peter at the closing of His ministry on earth. Jesus said to Peter in Luke 22:32, "I have prayed for you, that your faith should not fail." Jesus knew that failure is linked to faith, or the lack thereof, so that if one's faith fails, one fails. If we do not get hold of the lessons from I AM about the power of I AM, if we do not apply the principle of I AM and the faith of I AM to our present situations, we will never realize our dreams, even worse, never realize God's dreams for us.

Actually, there is a record of the same scenario for Jesus as for John with regard to who he was. This time Jesus is asking the question in Matthew 16:13: "Who do men say that I the Son of Man, AM?" Of course, like the others, some said all kinds of names. Jesus then asked the disciples in verse 15, "But who do you say that I AM?" Simon Peter answered in verse 16 and said, "You are the Christ, the Son of the living God." That "you are" declaration from Peter regarding the I AM of Jesus resulted in the two foundation stones on which "the church of Jesus Christ" was built and will be sustained: one, that the declaration was as a result of revelation from God the Father, and two, the statement itself as to who Jesus is.

There was a Roman centurion who came to Jesus looking to get his servant healed. He made the request to Jesus and Jesus responded with, "I will come and heal him." The centurion answered and said, "Lord, it is not necessary that you should come under my roof. But only speak a word and my servant will be healed, for I AM a man under authority, having soldiers under me." The centurion went on to explain how he commanded the soldiers and they obeyed him, and for this Jesus commended the centurion for having great faith. Jesus then told the centurion, "Go your way, as you have believed, so let it be done for you" (Matthew 8:5-13).

The Roman centurion's belief system for which he was commended came in three I AM forms. First, I AM not authorized with the same command abilities as Jesus. Second, I AM fully understanding of the principle of authority and command. Third, I AM fully convinced that with Jesus' authority in His realm, all He has to do is speak and His authority will heal my servant. Awesome.

~ JESUS, the "I AM" ~

LAST DAYS

Concerning the last days, the closing of the age, the end of the world as some would call it and a topic that is very intriguing to many, Jesus first said in Matthew 24:4, "watch out that you are not deceived." The first and most important criterion for understanding last days is that deception will be rampant, so be watchful, be careful. Jesus said many will come saying the time is drawing near; He said do not follow them. He also said in the same context that many will come saying, "I AM Christ" (Verse 5). That can be taken two ways: either they will come proclaiming that they themselves are Christ, which can be easily dismissed since He, Jesus, never promised to come to a pulpit or in secret, but as He left, in the sky for all to see. The other interpretation can be that many will come acknowledging that He is Jesus, He is Christ, just another tense for I AM. However, acknowledging Jesus as I AM or that Jesus is Christ is not sufficient. He left many other criteria concerning those who follow Him, character being paramount on that list. This reminds me of another "I AM" statement Jesus made when He told His disciple, "I AM among you as the One who serves" (Luke 22:27). Of course, the opposite of one who serves is one who is served, or maybe this can be interpreted as one who takes rather than one who gives.

In understanding I AMness, seeking truth as to the power of I AMness, we can reflect on Jesus when sought after in the garden of Gethsemane. The soldiers came to arrest Him, asking for Jesus of Nazareth; when He responded with, "I AM He," they drew back and fell to the ground (John 18:6). Powerful words, I would say. Actually, the original Hebrew text has no "He," so all He really would have said was "I AM."

PURPOSE and DESTINY

It was not too long after the garden incident when He was standing before Pilate and said, "I AM a king, for this cause I was born" (John 18:37). These are bold words; sure sounds like crazy lyrics from a man with no signs of a kingdom and no attributes of a king (as they expected it to be). This is the confidence of a man who knew who He was, what He was born for, where He was going, and had a full understanding of the power of I AM.

I have always held to the fact that when you search for success, you should look to someone who has achieved; of course, the greater the achievements the greater the challenge. I AMness was the driving force behind the success of Jesus Christ: He called things that were not as though they were, He spoke I AM in the present, and because of that the things He spoke about Himself became what He is. No other single individual has changed society, culture, history, individuals, etc., like Jesus Christ. He liberated women, He elevated children, He eliminated discrimination and racism, He transformed criminals, He respected authority. Jesus Christ, without arms and or ammunition, without academic degrees, with terrible odds against Him from birth, has had time divided between before Him and after Him.

When Jesus was referred to as the author and finisher of faith, the context was to fix your eyes on Him, or look unto Him (Hebrews 12:2). The Greek word used for *author* really means "chief leader," and that He did in leading the way of faith, leading the way in operating out of I AM. Of course, the second part is as important as the first because His finishing allows for the perfect example He set for us to follow. If He can, then you can too.

I have always said that the three most important words Jesus Christ ever said were "IT IS FINISHED" (John 19:30). His leadership and His completion and fulfillment of His objectives leave us with the perfect example of the application of the principle of I AM for accomplishing.

It is my humble opinion that we have the perfect I AM mentor in Jesus Christ. I would desire that all of us would get to the end of life and be able to say with confidence the words He said. *"I have brought You glory on earth, Father, by finishing what You gave Me to do" (John 17:4).*

Chapter Six
The "I AM" That Are Sons

<u>BECAUSE I AM A SON OF GOD, I AM WHO HE IS.</u>

> "As many as received Him,
> to them He gave the right
> to become children of God,
> to those who believe in His name."

<u>INHERITANCE</u>

In God the I AM, we saw where God is not exclusive to His principles but shares them with His sons. In Jesus the I AM, we saw Him exercising this principle and accomplishing His destiny. Now we look at others who realized they could and did because they understood and spoke and implemented I AMness.

Our successes at the tasks we have ahead of us are all dependent on us embracing and implementing the I AM that we are. I AM in its truest form is the manifestation of sonship.

Please see and hear this emphatically: "sons" does not have a gender; this is not about a male person but about all who become children of

~ I AM therefore I CAN ~

I AM being called sons.

We can look and learn from John the Baptist as a man who knew what he was about when he was asked, "Are you the Christ or Elijah?" He answered, "I AM not." When asked, "Who are you? What do you say about yourself?" John answered not with what his name was as we might do, but answered in accordance with truth, his calling, that which was his destiny. "I AM the voice of one crying in the wilderness: 'Make straight the way of The Lord,' as the prophet Isaiah said" (John 1:19-23). Imagine being so sure of who you are and what you are about to respond to a prophecy of hundreds of years past as the one presently fulfilling that said prophetic word. John answered no to something he would never be in the two persons they suggested or thought he might be. He did answer "I AM" to the situation as it pertained to his role in life and that which he was mandated to accomplish and which he did. Incidentally, John the Baptist was recognized and acknowledged by Jesus in Matthew 11:11 as being the greatest among men born of women, obviously not inclusive of Himself, of course, since John himself says of Jesus that He is greater than I (John 1:15,27&30).

Let us look at I AM and sonship as explained and taught by Jesus using the "prodigal son" story that we all know in Luke 15:11-32. Let me first say here that *Oxford* says prodigal means "recklessly wasteful." This is very important in understanding I AM, sonship, and the prodigal story.

We have one Father and two sons. The younger of the two sons asked the father for his inheritance; in other words, he said to the father, "I AM wanting what is mine from you now." The father then divided his livelihood BETWEEN them; in other words, he shared out his possessions to THEM, both sons. The younger son got his share of the father's estate that was his, gathered his belongings, and departed from the father. He journeyed to a far country and there, wasted his possessions with prodigal living; that is, he was recklessly wasteful with that which he had inherited. When he had spent all of his inheritance, a famine came and he was in want, so he linked up with someone from the country he was in as a servant feeding pigs.

~ The "I AM" That Are Sons ~

He was hungry to the point of wanting even what the pigs were eating, but even that was not offered to him. Finally, he came to himself, he saw the light, he came to his senses and remembered (not how well he was fed as a son) how well fed his father's servants were. He decided he had had enough so he was going back to the father to confess how stupid he had been, how recklessly wasteful he was, and ask the father for a job as a servant. On his way to the father long before he arrived, the father saw him, had compassion for him, and ran and kissed him saying, "This my son was dead and is alive again, he was lost and is found." The father gave him the best robe, a ring, sandals, killed a fatted calf, and made merry for his son had come back home.

The younger son represents one who is quick to exercise independence and to show how capable he is without the father. He lived his own I AM separate from his inherited destiny. He joined himself to outsiders in desperation and even in his dire need and wonton hunger received not even pig food from them. He finally saw the true picture and said, "I AM going back home to where I AM loved and respected and even though I AM no longer worthy to be called a son, not necessarily worthy to receive anything more, I AM thankful for whatever little I receive."

Please understand that the father in this lesson represents Father God, the great I AM, a Father who is willing to share His belongings with His sons, no demands before the fact and no questions or condemnation after the fact, a show of unconditional love. A father who is generous, faithful, forgiving, and totally supportive.

The older son now came onto the scene. He was coming in from the field and he heard music and dancing, so he inquired of a servant as to what was going on and learned of his brother's return. Unlike the father, this son did not rejoice but on the contrary he was very angry and refused to go into the house. The father came out to him and pleaded with him. The son answered and said to the father, "These many years I have been serving you, I never transgressed your commandment at any time and yet you never gave me a young goat that I might make merry with my friends, but as soon as this son of yours came, who has devoured your livelihood with harlots, you killed the fatted calf for him." This older son had learnt nothing of I AM from the father, although he had been with him all these years.

Contrary to the father's character, he was angry, bitter, selfish, vindictive, and unforgiving. Like the younger son he lived his own I AM, but right in the presence of the father, he was as "prodigal" as his younger brother. The younger went out and wasted his inheritance, while the older stayed at home and wasted his. The truth is that they both were recklessly wasteful with true inheritance, inheritance that surpasses finances, belongings, property, servants, etc. They both neglected to tap in from the father the lessons of the principles of I AM and therefore did not live out their "I AM" destiny, but instead chose to live their own prodigal I AM.

If we miss the dynamics of I AM and the potential it has to transform our lives, we miss the very essence of who God is and what He expects from His sons.

TRUE SONSHIP

Then there is the ultimate son in the person of Jesus Christ who learnt from His Father, as it says in John 5:19. He only does and says what He sees and hears from the Father and concludes by saying in John 16:15, "all that the Father has is mine." This is the major fact that the older prodigal son missed the fact that all that the father had was his; the father had already divided and shared his livelihood/belongings between his two sons. The younger son went off with his share so what was remaining was all belonging to the older son; the young goat he blamed the father for never giving him was already his. The older son appeared to be something he was not; he missed the boat entirely waiting for something he already had. How many of us are still today asking the Father for what He has already assigned to us? So many of us continue to ask the Father for what He has already divided and shared out to us. It is ironic that the Greek word for *sin* commonly explained as missing the mark also means to not have a share. The sin of missing the "I AM" principle will cause you to not have a share in God, and consequently miss all that you can be and do.

When the disciples of Jesus asked Him to teach them how to pray, the first principle He laid down was that you and I share the same Father; that's why He said, "Our Father." If we share a common father, then we share a common inheritance; we receive from the father all that the father has and is. Of course, that also includes I AM genes and DNA. So if Jesus and I share the same Father, then we both draw from the same gene pool and our lives have a parallel.

Wow, the awesomeness of being born again, born of God, born from above, born of a new Father, born of one who is Himself the great I AM.

INDIVIDUAL SONSHIP

There are many among us today like the young prodigal son. We all can see them and are quick to talk about them because their sin is obvious, as they have gone out from the Father and lived recklessly wasting their inheritance. However, it is a lot harder to identify the ones who stay at home, still present with the Father (or so it seems) yet not functioning with any level of understanding as to what they have inherited and the I AM that they are able to live out now. This is why we must set our eyes on Jesus, the chief leader and perfecter of faith, the one who calls things that are not as though they are, the one who lives I AM, the son of God.

This like Paul telling Timothy in his second book 4:6, "I AM already being poured out as a drink offering, and the time of my departure is at hand. I have fought the good fight, I have finished the race, I have kept the faith." Paul from day one on his Damascus road conversion, having met with the great I AM, was constantly focused on fulfilling his destiny for the kingdom of God. Paul clearly understood and was very sure of his calling and election; he was told of his mission to the Gentiles, and he was prepared to embrace his trials and challenges.

~ I AM therefore I CAN ~

Incidentally, success is measured not by one's opinion of success, not by the norms of success, but by accomplishing the will of God for your particular life. There have been many successful apostles since Jesus Christ and Paul who did not have the same fate to contend with. The same apostle, Paul, said in 1 Corinthians 15:10, "By the grace of God I AM what I AM. Paul understood that his particular ministry was not necessarily to be compared with that of a Peter, John or anyone else for that matter."

Beyond all the things we can do and become, that is the bottom line: live your own I AM, be your own person. I am reminded of the old adage, "The will of God will never take me where the grace of God cannot keep me." Our I AM is a personal living out of our individual calling and election. Be sure you know your calling, your giftings, your talents, your abilities, what you are about and who you are. Your I AM is dependent on you being absolutely sure and confident and knowing who you are. Then there is your election, where you are elected to function with the abilities, etc., that you are empowered with. This is about place and season/timing and not simply about talents and competences.

I AMness here on earth is the ultimate challenge in this apprenticeship life we live in the flesh as human beings. Our destiny, the very things we are designed and put here on this planet to accomplish, may differ from person to person, but living it from an I AM perspective is the only way to fulfillment.

When confronted with the possibility of being sent to Jerusalem to stand trial and the consequences that he might incur, even being bound or killed, Paul said, "I AM ready." There is a man sure of his commitment, his conviction, and the consequences that can follow. Paul declared in another scene, "I AM persuaded." To be successful in life, to be successful in completing and fulfilling our individual callings, one has to be in a state of I AM readiness and I AM "persuadedness" (yes, I know that is not a word; you get the point though). The root word of faith is *persuasion*.

In a speech to a number of Romans, Paul told them, "I AM debtor to

Greeks and barbarians, to the wise and the unwise." Paul knew he owed everyone the opportunity to hear him, consider what he had to say, and to arrive at their verdict. He continued by saying, "I AM ready to go to Rome also if that is what it would take to fulfill my calling and complete my debt." In summing up the context of what he was talking about. Paul says in Romans 1:16, "I AM not ashamed of the good news of Christ for it is the power of God to salvation for everyone who believes." A little further on in his deliberation in Romans 8:38-39, Paul says, "I AM persuaded that neither death nor life, nor angels, nor principalities, nor powers, nor things present nor things future, nor height nor depth, nor any other created thing shall be able to separate us from the love of God which is in Christ Jesus our Lord." Here is another man who knew precisely and accurately who he was, what he was about, and was certainly not compromising for anything. He was always prepared and ready to make his "I AM" declarations, and consequently his "I AM not" declarations.

THE COUNTERFEITERS

There are in every walk of life people and institutions that teach ways to manipulate the principles of God for selfish gain and personal achievement. We must be careful to avoid foolish, empty, and temporary gratification of an eternal principle with eternal benefits.

Here is an example taken from a counterfeit to the Godly principle: "The Law of Attraction tells you that whatever you think or say in the 'I AM...' form will be attracted to you. Whenever you say 'I AM this or that...' or think the same way, you will attract that into your life. The 'I AM' statement attracts the energies out of the Quantum Ocean (Mind of God) and into your aura. Therefore, using the Rune FA and the Laws of Quantum Physics, the Laws of Attraction, and the 'I AM' statements listed below, you will attract money into your life."

If that were true, I would be like most men inundated with women, riches, etc. I have worked the "laws of attraction" only to be disappointed by not being attractive or attracting enough. I still do not have the Jaguar and the estate I have been attracting for over fifty years now. The "I AM" we are discussing here is bigger than some metaphysical, quantum physical "law." This is not about half truths and formulas to tap into for some selfish gain. This is about knowing who WE ARE (plural of I AM).

Another charlatan of the truth says, "When you were putting those I AM statements out there, the Universe was listening! You used your 'I AM' statements to create your reality." While it is true that the universe can listen, it is important to understand that the universe listens only to one who has the authority to demand from it or command it. Only to one who has been given authority and one who exercises that authority over it. Further, more reality is very different from truth, and therefore anyone can create their reality. The resources you have and the things that pertain to your life are very real. However, the truth goes way deeper than what is seen, what is tangible, or what is even now present in anyone's life. The reality is I look very much like the average man walking the streets of earth; the reality is that you can only judge me by what you see and hear from me. The truth, however, is I AM way more than average, I AM far more capable than average, and I AM positioned a lot higher than the average; that's a fact. That is truth but does not necessarily surface with my reality. Reality is most often observed while truth is substantially deeper. It can be very true that a woman is pregnant yet reality can well say she is not.

I AM is not your spiritual name or a name you give yourself; I AM is the essence of who you are when you get linked to the great I AM. I AM is not some response to a metaphysical phenomenon; I AM does not refer to the spark of the divine that is at the core of your being or any other lyrics that suggest some religious dynamic. I AM is the core of your being when your being is connected to the true Divine one who Himself is the great I AM. The truth is you only have any potential of I AMness or manifesting your I AM when the source of your very being is rooted in God Almighty, the original and great I AM.

~ The "I AM" That Are Sons ~

In keeping this real, let us please understand that our "I AM" statements must be in keeping with what is truth. This is not being I AM for the sake of being I AM. This is not about being I AM to attract money and things and people into our life; this is about being I AM in the context of fulfilling your God-given and God-driven destiny. An example of this is found in Jesus' words in Revelation 3:14-22 to the church in Laodicea at the end of the age where they were saying, "I AM rich, I AM wealthy and I AM in need of nothing." While this might have been true given their visible reality and physical circumstances, they were told by Jesus that they did not know that they were "wretched, miserable, poor, blind and naked." Ouch!

The truth does truly hurt when you understand the difference between reality and truth. The reality was that the Laodiceans were looking good, and everything they said about their situation might have been very real. They probably had every proof that they were very rich, wealthy, and needed nothing. However, the truth of the matter was quite different from the way they saw it and I AM sure how most people around them saw it. Truth goes way deeper than what is observed on the surface. Truth has its roots in the eternal purposes of God. While it can include being rich, wealthy, and lacking nothing like King Solomon did (and God had no problem with him), it's about a much greater purpose.

The bottom-line conclusion, as a son we are mandated to live as our Father desires and as our big brother Jesus Christ did. "His divine power has given us ALL that we need for LIFE and GODLINESS" (2 Peter 1:3). Yes, we can.

Chapter Seven
The Thoughts of "I AM"

<u>WHETHER YOU THINK YOU CAN
OR THINK YOU CANNOT,
YOU ARE RIGHT.</u>

"As a man thinks in his heart, so is he."

THE BEGINNING

In this chapter on the thoughts of I AM, we will look at many things that we might have touched on in the previous chapter. This is how one begins to become "I AM." After all, becoming begins with objective. Like the "stop smoking" campaign that says, "Think, Talk, Quit," the objective is to stop smoking and the beginning of the process is with thoughts.

Every great accomplishment always began with a thought.

To become can also be interpreted or mean to begin to be, so the beginning of becoming is the beginning of I AM. Like God telling us, "we have the mind of Christ" (1 Corinthians 2:16) and "Be holy, for I AM holy" (1 Peter 1:16). And again, "Be perfect as I AM perfect" (Matthew 5:48). We are challenged continually to be like God, an awesome daunting task but obviously doable. Why would He say to be if we cannot be? I AM knows the I AM we are capable of being; He knows that we can.

The thoughts of I AM begin with I AM Himself and thinking like Him who is the great I AM, the very personification of I AMness. Our connection with I AM gives us the capacity to think I AM and consequently be I AM. To others not connected, not living in union, He says, "My thoughts are not your thoughts, nor are your ways My ways, for as the heavens are higher than the earth, so are My ways higher than your ways and My thoughts than your thoughts" (Isaiah 55:8).

So how do you become I AM? Is becoming I AM a simple process? Is becoming I AM time-consuming? Is becoming I AM guaranteed? There are many questions we can ask concerning I AM and the fulfilling of this in any of our lives. The first thing we need to know is that becoming anything that is worth something will take time.

Becoming must also have a beginning, continuity, and a conclusion. I think of God telling Jacob to not fear but go down to Egypt, for I, God, will make of you a great nation there. What? In enemy territory, in hard times, in slavery/bondage? A resounding yes. A handful of people went down to Egypt, actually just one family, and a nation of millions came out four hundred years later. If you know the story, you will know that most of them did not get the lessons on I AM they were meant to learn, and consequently suffered for it. However, Joshua and Caleb got it and were the leaders of those who had their minds in I AM mode; they were those who agreed that the land was theirs for the taking. "WE ARE (plural of I AM) able to take this land of Canaan" was their response to the cry for possession of the Promised Land.

"My mind is challenged not by my inadequacies, but by my capabilities."

So the question is, how did they become I AM? How do I become I

AM? How does anyone become I AM? The answer is obvious; the answer is simple. Simply by beginning to I AM, and everything in life begins with a thought.

THE MIND and THOUGHTS

Before we go any further and get all caught up in thinking we are somebody special and becoming I AM is going to make me superior, let's keep the balance by remembering that anything and everything any of us will ever become is for God, His purposes, and His kingdom.

I AM begins with a renewal of the mind, I AM continues when you make the non-I AM thoughts obedient to the I AM thoughts, and I AM becomes your heart and who you are when you constantly think I AM thoughts. You must begin to I AM, continue to I AM and constantly I AM.

Thought is the beginning of everything. Thought is the seed that gives birth to the greatest of inventions. Thought is at the root of every ideology, every idea, every plan, and every design. Like God in Genesis 1 when He says, 'let us make man in our image and likeness,' it was a thought He had before the actual creation of man began. Maybe then we can understand why He says in Romans 12:2 to renew your mind so that you will know His will. He also says in 2 Corinthians 10:5 to bring every thought obedient to Christ, and in another place, 'as a man thinks in his heart so is he.' So the beginning of I AM begins by beginning to I AM in your thoughts.

Let us be perfectly honest with each other: it is not easy to begin to I AM with our thoughts the way they presently are. We have been patterned after a world system that is driven by marketing and monetary gains; let's face it, we have been cloned. We have been socialized and cultured according to the whims and fancies of others, and most of us have been stripped of any individuality. As if that was not enough to retard and destroy us, we are surrounded daily with negative, selfish, and insecure people. We are forced to interact with troubled people who are threatened by the slightest show of, or perception of security, stability, and individuality. Just try being totally positive in your speech, answer "How are you? with "I AM great (or excellent)," reach out to someone, offer a helping hand, say "I AM here to help you," share something of yours, say "I AM here to serve you," and people will look at you like you are an alien. They might love it but not know how to handle it. You are not the alien; the concept is what is alien.

So we begin to become I AM by beginning to I AM. We begin to I AM by bringing our thoughts in line with I AM.

So start thinking of all the things you have always thought of being, of doing, your passions, your dreams. Think of all the ideas you have always thought of implementing or creating, all the things you would like to do for the kingdom of God; think of all the places you always thought of visiting; think of all the items you always dreamed of owning, your longings. All the thoughts that have been your hidden desires and dreams, the thoughts of being a way better person than you presently are. All the thoughts you thought you would never ever accomplish, bring them to the fore, move them forward, and place them on the front burners. Now write them down, analyze them, scrutinize them, being very sure it is what you want, and in essence, who you are. Just do it, you can.

Like Paul told the Philippians in 4:8, "whatever things are true/truthful, whatever things are noble/honorable, whatever things are just/right, whatever things are pure/clean, whatever things are lovely/acceptable, whatever things are of good report/well sounding, if there is any virtue/purity and if there is anything praiseworthy/commendable, think on these things." If we would think on these things, the answers and actions we respond with in any given situation will be far better ones. If we would think before we move, if meditation comes before reaction, we will surprisingly have way more success. Most of the problems we face in life are a direct result of our own mindlessness. We act, behave, and respond without any conscious thought or analytical dissecting of situations or circumstances before us.

~ The Thoughts of "I AM" ~

"Your successes or failures
will be determined
by what you set your thoughts on."

Becoming is a process that begins with our thoughts, continues with our thoughts, and is constantly about our thoughts. Only when we get that first thought pattern issue dealt with can we then move on to the implementation of the I AM thoughts and then move beyond. Thoughts are like the seed of a great tree: only after planting and nurturing and with the passage of time is there ever going to be the result of the seed and proof that the seed was indeed the tree that you desired. While seeds are recognizable to some experts, the only true proof of their substance, the only true worth of any seed is the final product.

When we set our mind in a certain direction, obviously the direction we would want to go, it is important that we keep it set on the things that can take us there.

Our destination will ultimately be determined by what we set our mind on.

CREATING PERCEPTIONS

I think of a tree that is set partly in shade and how it leans towards the sun, as if it is set on reaching the sun. The tree knows the sun is an important player in its destiny so it sets its sights on it. We talk a lot about mindset, and if I am right, probably more so in a negative sense. Regarding the person who does something wrong or behaves in a distasteful manner, we are quick to say that the root of their operation might be a mindset, and quite usually it is. However, the same is also true about the person who gets it right and operates in a positive manner. Many times in life the principles we hold as dear are operative in both the positive and negative realm, like my favorite analogy concerning the training of children. When we are told to train a child in the way he should go and when he is old he will not depart from it, usually we see it as biblical and therefore pertaining to proper training. However, when we fail to train or train badly, the same principle applies and the untrained or badly trained child will also not waver and consequently operate out of what was not received.

> "Your life must be a result of your thinking,
> not your thinking a result of your life."

Stop for a minute and focus on how much thinking we do. Constantly from the time we awake, there are thoughts on the day ahead, the day gone by, the tasks to be done, people to meet, things to see and do, etc. Now while you are stopped and focusing, look at how much of our thinking is unproductive, frivolous, and unnecessary. There is no doubt that we think a whole lot; however, more importantly is what we are thinking and what contribution it is making to our development. Sure enough I AM thinking, but am I thinking thoughts that enhance my I AM destiny? Are my thoughts the thoughts that are pulling my I AM from the future to the present? This is the real question.

My wife and I were counseling a newly wed couple recently, and after listening for quite a while, I realized the major problem was in the thinking. Constantly I heard from both parties, "I thought he was..." or "I thought she would..." None of their decisions were based on concrete evidence but rather on thoughts that were not necessarily true.

How many times in life have we judged situations wrongly because we thought rather than knew?

Much of life is manipulated by thought patterns that instigate buying patterns, brand choices, etc. Marketing gets its strength from causing you to think that one product is superior, of better quality, more reliable, etc. Even politicians manipulate you to perceive one as better, or more capable than the other. The world has understood that perception is all it takes to overrule truth and dismiss that which is right. I immediately think of the theory of evolution, the only theory that I know that is purported to be absolute truth. Without any concrete proof and with much scientific evidence opposing it, evolution is taught as fact rather than theory. All of this is done through establishing perceptions and creating thought patterns that support the product, candidate, theory, etc.

Experts say one of the major pitfalls of thinking and thoughts is prejudice, how many times we can wrongly judge situations and people based on our flawed perceptions and our personal prejudices.

I AM thoughts that will deliver you to your destiny have no limitations and no boundaries. I AM thoughts that are potent and capable are based on truth, the whole truth, and nothing but the truth.

I AM thoughts have the greater power to transform your perceptions; with I AM thoughts constantly dominating your mind, you will see yourself as the person you really are. I AM thoughts will make you more confident and cause you to be over the circumstances rather than under the circumstances. I AM thoughts will trigger change in your countenance and comportment. I AM thoughts will improve your entire life. Remember, as a man thinks in his heart so is he. Your thinking will determine your every mood and move; I AM thinking has the potential to pull you up from where you are now to where you ought to be. I AM thinking will cause your "cannot" to become "I can."

The potential for releasing your I AM and realizing your God-given destiny all begins with your thoughts. I can change my thoughts, you can change your thoughts, we can change our thoughts. Yes, we can.

Chapter Eight
The Words of "I AM"

<u>STICKS AND STONES MAY BREAK MY BONES
BUT WORDS CAN BREAK ME COMPLETELY.</u>

"The word is near you,
in your mouth and in your heart,
that is the word of faith which we speak."

THE CATALYST

While thoughts are extremely powerful and are usually expressed in words, the words are that which is heard and consequently the catalyst for decisions and assumptions.

We have all grown up with the cliché, "Sticks and stones will break my bones but words cannot hurt me." Nothing in life is further from the truth. Every one of us can attest to the absolute fact that somewhere in our lives, words have hurt us deeply. If the truth be known, words can hurt more deeply and cause more damage than any stick or stone usually does. This gives good reason for the words of Proverbs 18:21: "the power of life and death is in the tongue." While negative words have the potential to bring great damage to our lives, so also is the fact that positive encouraging words equally have the potential to bring great joy and peace to our lives.

The words you and I speak can either bring life or death. The tongue is a small member of the body, but like the rudder of a ship, it can steer tons in any direction. In other words (no pun intended), the words of "I AM" can either be used for or against you; your "I AM" words can either bring you life or death.

Check this: "I say to you that for every idle word men may speak they will give account of it in the day of judgment" (Matthew 12:36). That is how serious your words are, life or death, and accountability for every word said. That is why your "I AM" better be in keeping with that which is right, that which brings life, and that which will not bring harsh judgment. This principle is a serious one and somewhat scary given the quantity of words we speak in a lifetime and how many of them can be idle.

THE MANTRA

Having been a dabbler in Eastern philosophy back in the seventies, when that was the thing to do, I tried every guru and recited many mantras hoping to find some understanding of God.

I always joke about my favorite mantra, "owa tana siam," which certainly never got me connected to any god. However, I am appalled at the idleness of my words when I found out the truth of my declarations. No wonder I was so messed up; what else can happen if I AM constantly reciting, rehearsing, and reiterating, "Oh what an ass I AM"? Thank God I found my way out of that mess and now my I AM words are in keeping with my I AM purpose and my I AM destiny.

All your I AM's of the future are with you right now in your thoughts and in your words; you create the I AM that you will be by what you "I AM" now.

~ The Words of "I AM" ~

Remember Muhammad Ali: he said "I AM the greatest" long before he really even knew he was the greatest.

Words create, words have creative power, think of a word and immediately you see that image in your head. The next step is to move it from your head to tangible, present, now, reality, the power of I AM words to create your future.

CHOICE WORDS

Choosing I AM words and enhancing your I AM vocabulary begins with thinking I AM thoughts. Before you can speak I AM words, you must think I AM thoughts, and I AM thoughts come only from serious meditation on the person that you are and the purpose for which you exist. Because of socialization and the shaping that takes place in each of our lives, we are most times a long way off from who we really are. "Who I AM" and "who I have become and presently live out" can be worlds apart because of the cloning and patterning that we have been inundated with. Each one of us must find our true I AM and begin immediately to speak it into being; we have got to call things that are not as though they are. That is the essence of I AM.

Jesus gives a teaching about seeds and sowing them in a field and then explains to His disciples that words are like seeds: they take root, grow, and eventually produce a crop/fruit. Positive I AM words will bring about a harvest of the I AM that is latent in you. John writes about the power of the word in his gospel; he says, "In the beginning was the word and the word was with God and the word was God. He was in the beginning with God. All things were made through Him/The Word and without Him nothing was made that was made" (John 1:1-3). Then John continues in 1:14 and says, "And the word became flesh and dwelt among us…" The truth of what is being said here is the power of the word to produce when sown, the power of the word to become flesh, or to be transformed from invisible to visible.

~ I AM therefore I CAN ~

Remember in Genesis, God said "let there be and there was." God spoke a non-tangible word and a very tangible universe was produced. The principle still remains the same today: to create and make visible the I AM that you are meant to be is dependent on your I AM words.

There are many sayings, proverbs, and clichés regarding words, and much has been written concerning words and the effect they can have on life. Almost every culture has given us word sayings that we can learn from. Information is only useful if implemented, and therefore all that we hear about words must be applied to life to derive any positive benefit.

<u>Here are some "word" sayings worth considering:</u>

"A wise man hears one word and understands two."

"Every word has three explanations and three interpretations."

"Words are the voice of the heart."

"Words are like bees, they have honey and a sting."

"Fine words butter no parsnips."

"The word which you keep between your lips is your slave, the word spoken out of season is your master."

"The words of the wicked are a deadly ambush, but the words of the upright rescues them."

"Better than a thousand hollow words is one word that brings peace."

"When you have spoken the word it reigns over you, when it is unspoken you reign over it."

"A word is like a stone let go, it cannot be recalled."

~ The Words of "I AM" ~

"A bad word whispered will echo a hundred miles."

I AM is subject to you speaking the words of I AM as you know they should be.

Too many times in life, we are living out I AM based on the perception of another who has spoken negative or assumptive I AM words into our lives. Most of us live the I AM that was spoken to us by parents and other authoritative figures in our lives. The consequence of this is becoming unstable, insecure, and immature, untrue I AM statements being made and hence declaring the wrong person that I AM and creating the wrong future of my "I AM."

Just today I was listening to a Christian radio station where a lady calling in, after much declaration of her faith, then said, "I AM a sinner" and further on, "I AM not perfect." How on earth can one be a saint and a sinner at the same time? How do we find it common lingo to say "I AM saved" among many I AM statements, but then switch to a number of negative I AM's after that, mingling seed?

TWO PATHS

When Jesus said, "you are either for Me or against Me," He divided life very simply into two categories with the choice totally and absolutely ours. He also said there is a narrow road and a broad road, darkness or light, head or tail, righteous or unrighteous, top or bottom, etc. The consequence of that is we also only have two belief systems, truth and false. The question is, which one are your words giving support to?

I AM a perfect example of this, having lived my formative years in the presence of negative, pessimistic people as the majority of the world is, and with many "leaders" who gave little or no encouragement. The results of hearing negative remarks and comments created an I AM for me that made me terribly insecure and consequently, extremely self-centered. The results of such a molding was an I AM that was founded on imagination and lies with

~ I AM therefore I CAN ~

a constant demand to draw the attention to me.

I remember one time meeting a family and telling them I AM half-Hawaiian. Well, it turned out the mother knew my dad and family, and being anything close to Hawaiian was a standing joke. Yes, it was embarrassing but I needed to be somebody, so I continued with my pseudo-life and my imaginative I AM words. I was in Germany on a training course once and it was great to be in a strange country where I could not speak the language, but when I did speak I was able to speak my I AM lies. I AM a prince, I AM an heir to an empire, I AM a star from the Caribbean, I AM this and that, and the lies went on. My I AM statements were based on movie characters, successful famous people, celebrities, etc. I lived in an imaginative world with no real understanding of who I was, where I came from, what I was doing here, or where I was going. I was for many years of my life an insecure, self-centered, hypocritical jerk.

On the subject of words, let me say this: I was living a lie because my I AM was based on perceptions and assumptions, all of which were from someone else's thoughts and words to me. When in my old age, sorry, my more mature age, I found out through my love for words and their meaning, the meaning of the word *education*, and things changed. Education in most part is perceived and delivered as information being passed on from one who has to one who has not. However, the root of the word *education*, which is *educere*, means "to lead out, to bring out, or to draw out." Hence, educating someone is not about putting in anything but about drawing out what is already there.

The "I AM" I was living out back then was not me; it was not who I was designed and destined to be. My true I AM was latent and buried beneath the I AM created for me by people and society, which caused me to be an absolute mess.

~ The Words of "I AM" ~

THE DAILY WORD

Have you ever thought of or paid attention to the quantity of I AM statements we make in one day and how absolutely normal it is to speak them without any concept of their delivery?

On any given day we could very well all say, "I AM tired, I AM starving, I AM unlucky, I AM broke, I AM fat, I AM ugly, I AM useless, etc." Then there are even worse statements like "I AM going to kill my wife if she doesn't have lunch ready on time" or "I AM going to die if I don't get to the bank on time and I AM sick and tired of this mess, etc." I AM sure you get the point. "I AM" words must reflect truth rather than reality.

I AM words create your future and deliver you to your destiny, so it is imperative that they are in keeping with who you really are and where you are going.

It is quite possible in reality to be physically tired, but the truth is given something exciting to do and all tiredness goes away as the adrenalin pushes it off. While we all get hungry, the majority of us have no idea what it really means to be starving. The bottom line is that we must watch closely our "I AM" statements, as they are creating for us our future. If you will be disappointed if lunch is not ready on time, then say so; it's hardly the reason to want to kill your loving wife who is creating a meal for you. Getting to the bank could be vitally important, but the truth be known it can be done another time and is hardly something to die for. Do something about dealing with the mess that is upsetting to you; no need to let it get you sick and tired. If you say you are sick and tired long enough, you better believe your words will deliver to you sickness and tiredness. The choice is yours: you can choose your words and in turn choose your future, and that future can be life or death.

I AM has power as a thought and certainly it begins there, but using I AM words that are in keeping with who you really are and where you are heading is the real source of delivery to your place of purpose.

~ I AM therefore I CAN ~

MONITORING WORDS

We have five sons and one grandson so the role of men, the words they speak, and their overall development is extremely important to us. I AM constantly monitoring music lyrics, television shows, etc., for the words that are shaping our young people. Sad to say, but most of it is not conducive to delivering them anywhere near to what they are meant to be. It is delivering them to a place, but not the place they are meant to be. It is in fact producing the crop that we are now faced with, a generation of gangsters, bad-boys and rebels. They are told by people like 50 Cent to "Get rich or die trying." Men who exchange the I AM of God for their lives and are reduced to referring to their women as female dogs. They replace "I AM" with "Me Are," which is slang for I AM, and sing into their heads constantly, "Me Are badboy, Me Are badboy nobody no tell me what to do, Me Are badboy, Me Are badboy."

In all fairness, there are many songs with good lyrics and there is even a category called "conscious music." This conscious music with more positive lyrics is not always top of the charts and not always from the more popular artists, however. I recall years ago one song that said you were a champion, and if you are a champion, then talk like a champion and walk like a champion.

Even long before I heard the champion song I remember Helen Reddy singing, I AM woman, I AM strong, I AM invincible. This song and its words no doubt had a great impact on many women of that era and their transition to a more positive I AM. If my observation is true, then maybe I can understand why women have risen to the heights they have in recent years and why men are where they are.

I thank God, literally, for it was only through Him that my life took on a new focus, a positive turn, and a thrust towards maturity, security, and destiny. He gave me a wife that constantly demands the best from me in word and deed; He linked me with people who were encouraging and with true leaders who sought to take me up from my present position constantly.

~ The Words of "I AM" ~

I now know that leaders can only take you where they have been themselves. Mindful of that, I AM always looking for the next level and the repositioning that is relevant to the now and the future that is to be.

All of the I AM that you are is presently with you. It's not put in there except by God and it is your responsibility to draw it out, speak it out, live it out now. The I AM that you are is far superior to the I AM that you are presently living out. Draw out the real I AM with the words of I AM. Yes, you can.

Chapter Nine
The Attitude of "I AM"

<u>ATTITUDE IS THE ONE THING
THAT WILL KEEP YOU LEVEL
AND TAKE YOU HIGHER.</u>

"Let the same attitude be in you
which was also in Christ Jesus."

<u>THE REAL DEAL</u>

I AM will begin with thoughts and cause the release of words, but will find its greatest fulfillment in attitude, a positive, progressive attitude.

Winston Churchill said, "Attitude is a little thing that makes a big difference."

Who I AM is best represented by my attitude. While my thoughts can be private and my words can be well constructed and executed, my attitude can make me or break me. "I AM" as an attitude will give your life great altitude. I AM is the real deal.

~ I AM therefore I CAN ~

We are all aware that words can be spoken with great volume and words do speak loudly, yet with all their volume and loudness, they can only say so much. We are all also confident that attitude and body language speaks volumes even in the absence of words. Therefore, your attitude can speak louder than your audible words and even contradict the lyrics and rhetoric we so easily spout.

Your attitude can speak louder than your words. A man is measured not by what he does but by how he does what he does.

The attitude of I AM will give your life more meaning than millions of wise and persuasive words. People see disabilities as the big obvious things in life; few see eye glasses as a disability, and even fewer see a negative attitude as the serious disability that it is.

Statistics say that attitude and personality are more responsible for employment selection than academics. I have this friend who holds a high position with a multinational corporation. This friend is always interviewing people for senior placements, and he is constantly refusing what he calls intellectual dunces. Employers are constantly looking for a personality fit with the particular organization and its present personnel. While many can easily present their academic accomplishments, few are able to market themselves with the right attitude, an "I AM" attitude can do this. I know of people who have been hired without any reference to their academics, skills, or past experiences; they were hired based on their countenance, comportment, attitude, and personality.

Society has duped us into thinking that academics alone is the do all and end all for job selection; we therefore have a vast number of unemployable individuals lacking severely in the attitude department. While academics is absolutely necessary and must be pursued at all cost, the only cost it should not surpass is that of a dynamic personality and attitude, an "I AM" attitude.

Your attitude can make you or break you, make you rise or cause you to fall; it's all about attitude. Attitude is like a balloon: it will rise or fall depending on what is inside, water or helium. If you do not like

~ The Attitude of "I AM" ~

something, then make every effort to change it; if for whatever reason you cannot change it, then by all means change your attitude towards it.

Albert Einstein says, "Weakness of attitude becomes weakness of character."

The attitude of I AM is an attitude that reflects your I AM thoughts and your I AM words, and finds its completion in your I AM personality.

The attitude of I AM is one of security, confidence, and focus.

The attitude of I AM has no place for insecurity, timidity, or double-mindedness.

The attitude of I AM presents itself as "I AM secure," "I AM confident," and "I AM focused."

Attitude is a little thing that makes a big difference.

Attitude is the one thing that can increase your altitude.

Attitude is best understood by how you "look at it dude."

Attitude is the way one looks at a situation or circumstance and consequently how one deals with the challenges it might offer.

Attitude will determine whether you are under the circumstances or over the circumstances. You can present the exact situation to any two people and you can get two diametrically opposing views. The results will be based on how each individual views the situation and as a consequence, the action they take in dealing with that particular situation. Attitude will always be determined by perspective. When your perspective is great then you attitude is great, when your perspective is positive then your attitude is positive. The proper perspective will always determine the proper attitude.

POSITIONING

An "I AM" attitude comes from one who fully understands their positioning in any given matter, and their rights and competencies to handle it effectively. Life is all about positioning; being in the right place is not enough if you are not in the right position. We all know of many instances that are referred to as being "in the wrong place at the wrong time," that's bad positioning. Place is general whereas position is precise and accurate. For you football fans, it's like being offside, being in the general vicinity of the goal but not accurately in the precise position. On a mango tree might be the right place to be for getting mangoes from a tree; however, if you are not positioned where the mangoes are, then you will miss the opportunity to maximize being on the mango tree.

I AM is being in the NOW; I AM positioning supercedes the matrix of time as we know it.

I AM as an attitude only comes from living constantly with I AM thoughts and speaking I AM words. You cannot live out an I AM attitude with non-I AM thoughts or non-I AM words. I AM thoughts give birth to I AM words, which in turn deliver an I AM attitude. I AM is conceived through I AM thoughts, birthed by I AM words, and delivers with an I AM attitude.

The apostle Peter tells us in his first letter in chapter two from verse 21, Christ left us an example that we should follow in His steps. "He committed no sin, no deceit was found in His mouth, when He was insulted He did not retaliate, when He suffered He made no threats. Instead He entrusted Himself to Him who judges justly." The bottom line is that He had the right attitude in all situations; He was over the circumstances rather than under them.

ATTITUDE DELIVERS

I challenge you to say positive "I AM" words about yourself right now and watch your attitude change. Positive I AM words repeated

~ The Attitude of "I AM" ~

right now as you head out the door will cause you to begin to think differently; you will walk differently, you will speak clearly and accurately, your countenance will get brighter, your confidence will increase, and your life will become an attraction. Watch people ask you what's different, what did you do to yourself; people can see that something is different. Try it, I AM confident it will work for you right now, so do it. I have proven it on both sides of the fence. I have deliberately gone out filled with I AM thoughts and words and seen the reaction to me from others. I have even had people who have known me for years remark how young I look, how bright, how great, etc., etc. Your countenance will change; your life will change.

I think of Cain, the brother of Abel and also the murderer of his brother Abel. Long before Cain decided to kill his brother. God recognized something was wrong and asked him, "Why are you angry? Why has your countenance fallen?" Cain's attitude was reflecting through his countenance: his face was downcast, he was angry, and his I AM thoughts led him to his I AM attitude and finally to taking his own brother's life.

An I AM attitude can cause you to be the son of God that you are and live it, while the wrong negative I AM operating in your life can result in your own demise. Cain suffered greatly for his wrong attitude. It's no different now, you will too. I AM has the potential to take you all the way up, but use of the same principle negatively will also take you all the way down.

Attitude is so important in your life, it is worth every effort you can make to improve it or develop it. There are so many people in life who have missed out big time from maximizing their greatness because of bad attitudes. There are sportsmen I know personally who never performed at the highest level because their attitude did not match their talents. The same can be said for every area of life; many have missed out completely because of bad attitudes.

One writer on attitude and its effects on people's lives says that using the word "power" to emphasize the effect of a positive attitude might seem like an overstatement. Yet, if you have been an observer of people and their behaviors, you have probably seen the effects of an attitude that is turned around that was so extraordinary that the word "powerful" would be the only way to describe it.

Attitude is a powerful dynamic in everyone's lives, and therefore it is very necessary that we do everything possible to ensure we have and operate with a right attitude.

THE LIFE GAUGE

I have always found it very interesting that a plane has an attitude gauge. I wonder how many of us would have performed way better had we had an attitude gauge to measure our performance. The levelness that is necessary to take us successfully forward is so crucial to our lives and our destiny. The attitude gauge in the plane determines its levelness, its balance, its stability, its on-course-ness, etc. A little off course at the beginning of a flight, if not corrected, allows for it being totally off course in a short period of time, and a final course to a wrong destination eventually.

I will never forget the first time I had the opportunity to take off on a flight in a single-engine plane. I thought I was the "cat's whiskers," feeling very proud of myself as we headed towards the open skies. The captain asked me where I thought the runway was that we had just left, and with all confidence I said, "Behind us, duhh," well not so rudely, of course, only to find out that the runway was almost at right angles with the plane because I had not focused on the attitude. When I thought I was going straight, the truth was I was slowly turning off course from the time we left the ground.

Check your life's attitude gauge because if you are off course now at the beginning of your journey, you will be way off course in a very short time. Point one degrees off now is likely to be one thousand degrees off down the road, so check your attitude gauge now and make the necessary corrections before you crash.

An attitude of gratitude will always give you fast altitude.

~ The Attitude of "I AM" ~

ATTITUDE IS KING

An unknown author writes the following and sums up the importance of attitude and particularly a great attitude, or an I AM attitude. "Attitude is more important than the past, than education, than money, than circumstances, than what other people say or do. It is more important than appearance, giftedness or skill. It will make or break a company, a church, a home. The remarkable thing is, we have a choice every day regarding the attitude we will embrace for that day. We cannot change our past. We cannot change the fact that people will act in a certain way. We cannot change the inevitable. The only thing we can do is play on the one string we have, and that is our attitude."

It is interesting that Bible scholars, while interpreting some translations, used attitude in place of spirit, like this one: "be made new in the attitude/spirit of your minds" (Ephesians 4:23). In another place they used attitude in place of mind: "your attitude/mind should be the same as that of Christ Jesus." Yet another place they said, "...arm yourselves also with the same attitude/mind..." You ask what's my point? Well, attitude absolutely begins with the mind and most definitely is linked to your spirit. The right mindset will create a right spirit and absolutely deliver a right attitude, an "I AM" attitude.

King Saul was the king of Israel, anointed and appointed by God to lead His people forward and upward. God's words to Saul through the prophet Samuel were, "...the Lord has anointed you commander over His inheritance." Further on in the same chapter 10 of 1 Samuel, verse 6, Saul is told by Samuel, "The Spirit of the Lord will come upon you, and you will prophesy with them and be turned into another man." Nothing changed physically for Saul at that moment or at any time in his life; what changed was his attitude. In verse 9 it says God gave Saul a new heart. Attitude is a spirit; I AM attitude is a spiritual principle and needs a new heart, a heart beating in sync with the greater I AM.

Then there is King David and his son King Solomon, also ordinary

~ I AM therefore I CAN ~

men whose attitudes were transformed when submitted to the great I AM.

Your attitude too can change. I AM has the potential to do that and cause your "I can" attitude to be released.

Chapter Ten
I AM the Finished Product

<u>THERE IS NO SATISFACTION
LIKE FINISHING A TASK PROPERLY</u>

> Jesus, knowing that all things
> were now accomplished,
> said,
> "It is Finished."

<u>TENACITY AND FORTITUDE</u>

Finishing is a very important concept in life and should be the focus of everyone. Here in Trinidad and Tobago, we have an expression for non-finishers, they are referred to as "hot and sweaty." This saying means they are of those who are quick to get started, might well show some zeal along the way, but are not known for finishing anything. While in the tropics here, most efforts require you to be hot and sweaty; there must be, along with the hot and sweaty, the tenacity to finish and get the job completed. Your I AM needs to be completed, accomplished, concluded, and finished; if your I AM is not finished, then you are an I AM not.

So finishing is vitally important, since it's the only way true success or accomplishment can be measured. However, finishing in what area of life is what needs to be addressed. You can finish school, you can finish a race, a project, an assignment, and many other things in life. Your I AM as a finished product must be your ultimate purpose.

Switzerland was very well known for its "Finishing Schools," which usually were for women but some did host men, more so the "elite" in society who wanted to be trained in cultural and social activities and the finer etiquette of protocol and life. Most, if not all, of these schools have closed since the mid-nineties as the finishing school concept has become less important to those who would have otherwise been interested in its use. "Finishing" is still a very important and necessary concept for every individual in the area of a person's development, and finishing one's I AM is the most important of all.

Another interesting concept of finishing is the procedure that single malt Scotch whisky undergoes whereby the spirit is matured in a cask of a particular origin and then spends time in a cask of different origin. Typically, the first cask is an oak cask formerly used to mature bourbon. The second cask is usually one that has been used to mature some sort of fortified wine, often sherry, though sometimes port or Madeira.

Of course, our I AM finishing totally involves quite a different Spirit. It is interesting to note, however, that the final product in the above procedure is not ready, complete, or accomplished until it is transferred from one cask to another of superior quality. In the same way, a radical transference must take place in your own mentality and life from the I AM that you think you are to the more mature I AM that you really truly are.

Everything in life that has any purpose, value, or significance should always be evaluated as a finished product. Nothing can be rightly judged without it having been completed, tested, and proved. Products are never evaluated or sold in their developmental stage, as children are not delivered in their embryonic phase; even prototypes

~ I AM the Finished Product ~

and concepts, as important as they are, only reflect desires and future expectations.

I AM is no different in this regard: the finished product must reflect the power and consequences of its application in the lives that have embraced and implemented the principles of releasing I AM.

I AM is not about future dreams and hopes. I AM is not about who or what I hope to be or even who I will be. I AM is about the NOW, I AM is about "be-ing," I AM is about who "I BE."

COUNTING THE COST

Fourteen years ago we were building the house we presently live in, and after a few months walls were up, the roof was on, steps were completed, and we could see and touch what was only a drawing previously. I remember getting all excited because it seemed to me the house was almost finished and money was still looking good. Then someone told me, "Wait until the finishing stage starts and the money is going to be flowing out real fast." Man, were they right. I never knew that the finishing took almost more money than the structural form that was in place. The same is true in our lives and finishing our I AM. The foundational work is crucial and most necessary; however, the I AM that is the finished product will cost more and can even take a longer period than the past work.

The principle of finishing is summed up in these words: "Which of you intending to build a building does not sit down first and count the cost, whether he has enough to finish it. Lest, after he has laid the foundation and is not able to finish, all who see it begin to mock him saying, 'this man began to build and is not able to finish'" (Luke 14:28-30).

THE FOUNDATION

Like Jesus asking His disciples, "Who do you say that I AM?" Peter remarked, "You are the Christ the Son of the living God." Then Jesus says, "Flesh and blood has not revealed that to you but My Father in heaven." Here we have the two most powerful dynamics of church building, those two statements being foundational on which to build. However, while we know the necessary foundation and hopefully it is laid, the finished product and its role from what started with an "I AM" question is very clear. The church that is built on this foundation as a finished product has access to hell because its gates cannot prevail against it. The gate that is holding people in sickness, in poverty, sin, oppression, crime, drugs, unrighteousness, etc. Every and any gate holding in people must be opened for the great I AM to release captives to fulfill their individual I AM (Luke 16:15-18).

In John 5:36 Jesus says, "I have a greater witness than John's, for the works which the Father has given Me to finish, the very works that I do bear witness of Me that the Father has sent Me." In the same way all that you do to finish your I AM must represent that which the Father has purposed you for.

THE CONCLUSION

One of Jesus' closing remarks is, "I have brought you glory on the earth. I have finished the work which You have given Me to do" (John 17:4). What satisfaction, what joy, what an accomplishment. One person said that the cemetery is the richest place on earth because in it are buried dreams, aspirations, ideas, inventions, arts and crafts, books, and songs that were never accomplished. Your I AM has a particular blueprint with your name on it. There are things in life that you have been wired for and programmed to do; if you do not get it done, it might very well never get done. Your I AM is your I AM and your I AM alone. You have an I AM that needs to be completed, accomplished, and finished; you have an I AM that you should be working diligently on right at this moment. Your "I can" will only follow your I AM.

The apostle Paul understood the concept of finishing his I AM and told his understudy Timothy, "I have fought the good fight, I have

~ I AM the Finished Product ~

finished the race, I have kept the faith" (2 Timothy 4:7). Paul had an I AM to complete that was his alone; he finished his I AM and brought God joy. You too have your own personal I AM that is yours alone to finish. It is not good enough to have started it; it is great that you are working on it, so please finish it. You can.

I have heard of many different sports where athletes who were excellent and strong in certain areas never realized their full potential because they had a poor finish. Improving on one's finish is a serious challenge for many because it is the finish that determines whether you are victorious or not. Your I AM is not just a brilliant start, and it is not a great effort; it will take a dynamic finish to accomplish your I AM.

We must recognize that there is a finished product that is expected by God. There is a role of the church, there is the function of the body, there is the expectation of saints, there is the position of the sons, and there is the readiness of the bride. All of these are one and the same entity with varying functions dependent on time, calling, office, seasons, etc. However, one undeniable fact is the criterion for accomplishment and acceptance. While much can be preached about a number of topics and numerous books can be written and read, the bottom line remains what The Father desires.

When, like Jesus, Paul, and many others, you can get to the end of your life here on earth and make declarations and remarks (with proof) that say you are finished, then you have finished your personal I AM. That is when you get the understanding that your strength brings your God joy. The joy of the Lord is your strength. Finishing your I AM is joy unspeakable and full of glory.

"I AM" is present tense singular person; that single person is you and who you are now presently.

I AM as a fulfilled product has no place for "might," "will," "could," or "should." I AM must deliver every individual who has implemented its principles to a place of "It is finished," an accomplished, complete individual. Your I AM must lead to "I can," and finally, "I did."

~ I AM therefore I CAN ~

I AM has as its ultimate conclusion the finished product, whose criterion is already set, spoken, documented, and eternally sealed.

I AM is ultimately imaging the great I AM.

I AM is ultimately being I AM on earth as I AM is in heaven.

I AM is the manifestation of sonship from a Father who is also I AM.

I AM is being pure, holy, perfect, and without spot or wrinkle.

I AM is being ready and prepared for the marriage of the Lamb.

I AM is being the glorious bride/church for a glorious groom/Lord Jesus Christ.

I AM is your ultimate purpose, objective, goal, and destiny.

I AM finished is joy unspeakable and full of glory.

THE "I AM" LIST

The following is a list of all that the believer and follower of I AM has been endowed with for the release of their own I AM. The spiritual DNA has been passed on from the Father to the Son to the Holy Spirit and finally to you. He is in you and you are in Him. There is no separation: you are intrinsically woven "twogether" with God; who He is, you are. He is I AM, therefore you are I AM.

So with total confidence and fullness of faith, you can say, "Who I AM is I AM" because who I AM is, you are, and who you are, is I AM. Who I AM is, I AM, and Who I AM, is I AM. Therefore, because I AM, I can.

Continually think I AM, speak I AM, be I AM, because you are I AM. Because you are I AM, then you can.

~ I AM the Finished Product ~

Release your I AM; finish your I AM.
Who I AM is, I AM.
Who I AM, is I AM.
I AM, therefore I can.
I AM that I AM.
I AM who I AM.
I AM saved.
I AM justified.
I AM born from above.
I AM born again.
I AM born of God.
I AM forgiven.
I AM forgiving.
I AM a son of God.
I AM one with God.
I AM an heir of God.
I AM a co-heir with Christ.
I AM righteous.
I AM recreated.
I AM a new creation.
I AM seated with Christ.
I AM holy.
I AM whole.
I AM perfect.
I AM right.
I AM the light of the world.
I AM the salt of the earth.
I AM love.
I AM a lover.
I AM gifted.
I AM a giver.
I AM a servant.
I AM wisdom.
I AM wise.
I AM truth.
I AM life.
I AM blessed.
I AM highly favored.

~ I AM therefore I CAN ~

I AM fearfully made.
I AM wonderfully made.
I AM the head.
I AM the top.
I AM rich.
I AM prosperous.
I AM more than a conqueror.
I AM capable.
I AM competent.
I AM able.
I AM obedient.
I AM a peacemaker.
I AM humble.
I AM comforted.
I AM a comforter.
I AM pure in heart.
I AM caring.
I AM mature.
I AM of great faith.
I AM faithful.
I AM a believer.
I AM a counselor.
I AM hopeful.
I AM the bride of Christ.
I AM willing.
I AM free, liberated, and emancipated.
I AM worship.
I AM praise.
I AM a sower.
I AM a harvester.
I AM a disciple.
I AM disciplined.
I AM anointed.
I AM rest/sabbath.
I AM knowledge.
I AM knowledgeable.
I AM understanding.
I AM committed.

~ I AM the Finished Product ~

I AM responsible.
I AM a priest.
I AM a mediator.
I AM special.
I AM consecrated.
I AM dedicated.
I AM purposeful.
I AM grateful.
I AM kind.
I AM gentle.
I AM self-controlled.
I AM godly.
I AM respectful.
I AM appointed.
I AM limitless.
I AM borderless.
I AM pure.
I AM in authority.
I AM blameless.
I AM spotless.
I AM submitted.
I AM submissive.
I AM a winner.
I AM patient.
I AM prepared.
I AM confident.
I AM sure.
I AM complete.
I AM finished.

<u>Who I AM, is I AM.</u>
<u>Who I AM is, I AM.</u>

<u>I AM, THEREFORE I CAN.</u>

<u>Sonship Realized.</u>

Synopsis

It is only right and appropriate, given the challenges that I AM might offer and the importance we place on the timing of this message, that a synopsis be presented for clarity and reference.

1. I AM must be approached as a concept of drawing the future into the present and of being and not just of doing. Yes, I can do, and yes, I can be.

2. I AM must have as its ultimate objective being an image of God on earth. Yes, I can be.

3. I AM can only be truly and fully accomplished through fellowship with the great I AM. Yes, I can.

4. I AM is living the essence of the Father, who is Himself already all of I AM. Yes, that I can.

5. I AM is following after (in the footsteps of) The Son Jesus Christ, who is a forerunner to sonship and I AMness. Yes, I can.

6. I AM is the release of one's individual personal sonship as it relates to the Father and the Son. Yes, I can.

7. I AM begins with thoughts that are in keeping with those that represent what the Father is thinking. Yes, I can do that.

8. I AM is about speaking constantly and continually words that

reflect the faith, confidence, and assurance of I AMness. I can do that.

9. I AM is the living out of the thoughts, words, and principles of I AMness in keeping with the attitude that I AM is. I can do that.

10. I AM is the fulfillment and completion of one's individual purpose and destiny from God. That I can and will do.

The Nova Group International
getting it right...

The Nova Group is a not-for-profit, nondenominational Messianic ministry. It was founded in 1999 with a passion for a practical, relevant, life-related approach to "God." "International" was added to the name in 2006.

> While our motto is <u>*getting it right....*</u>,
> we are also known as
> <u>"not the church you attend,</u>
> <u>but the church that attends to you."</u>

For many years prior to 1999, my wife and I, along with a few other people, constantly saw and heard much that disturbed us concerning "church," "Christianity," "God," "Jesus Christ," etc... We met many people disenchanted with religious and rigorous forms that were measured by quantity of bodies rather than quality of life. Many were in church but not in Christ.

We were mandated to do something about it and consequently adopted a whole different approach to ministry and the release of what we had to offer. We ultimately decided to be who and what God had created us to be and told us to do, and that nothing else mattered. This is the same desire we have for everyone else, for them to be the individual that they are designed to be and to take that to its destiny.

We work towards a community of people with a Nova/New mentality unrestricted by ethnicity, gender, culture, religion, or any other limiting element, people with a Christ-like attitude. Simply put,

<u>*A CHRIST-LIKE COMMUNITY,*</u>
<u>*LIMITLESS AND BORDERLESS.*</u>

This vision also gave birth to Step-Up International Academy, a private primary school that is now into its sixth year.

Contact Information

Telephone: 1 868 660 NOVA (6682)
Mobiles: 1 868 390 NOVA
1 868 474 NOVA

Mail: P.O. Box 430 Scarborough
Tobago,
Trinidad and Tobago,
West Indies

Website: www.tngi.org
E-mail: info@tngi.org

~ Notes ~

Printed in the United States
142347LV00001B/13/P